World Wisdom
The Library of Perennial Philosophy

The Library of Perennial Philosophy is dedicated to the exposition of the timeless Truth underlying the diverse religions. This Truth, often referred to as the *Sophia Perennis*—or Perennial Wisdom—finds its expression in the revealed Scriptures as well as the writings of the great sages and the artistic creations of the traditional worlds.

The Perennial Philosophy provides the intellectual principles capable of explaining both the formal contradictions and the transcendent unity of the great religions.

Ranging from the writings of the great sages of the past, to the perennialist authors of our time, each series of our Library has a different focus. As a whole, they express the inner unanimity, transforming radiance, and irreplaceable values of the great spiritual traditions.

The Foundations of Christian Art appears as one of our selections in the Sacred Art in Tradition series.

Sacred Art in Tradition

The aim of this series is to underscore the essential role of beauty and its artistic expressions in the Perennial Philosophy. Each volume contains full-color reproductions of masterpieces of traditional art—including painting, sculpture, architecture, and vestimentary art—combined with writings by authorities on each subject. Individual titles focus either on one spiritual tradition or on a central theme that touches upon diverse traditions.

The Foundations of Christian Art

Illustrated

Titus Burckhardt

Edited by
Michael Oren Fitzgerald

Foreword by
Keith Critchlow

World Wisdom

Cover image: South portal of the Church of Saint-Pierre, Aulnay, France, ca. 1130

Image research and book design by Susana Marín

Library of Congress Cataloging-in-Publication Data

Burckhardt, Titus.
  The foundations of Christian art : illustrated / Titus Burckhardt ; edited by Michael Oren
Fitzgerald ; foreword by Keith Critchlow.
      p. cm. -- (Sacred art in tradition series)
  Includes bibliographical references and index.
  ISBN-13: 978-1-933316-12-3 (pbk. : alk. paper)
  ISBN-10: 1-933316-12-8 (pbk. : alk. paper) 1. Christian art and symbolism--History. I.
Fitzgerald, Michael Oren, 1949- II. Title. III. Series.
  BV150.B86 2006
  246--dc22

                                                                    2005035159

Printed on acid-free paper in China.

For information address World Wisdom, Inc.
P.O. Box 2682, Bloomington, Indiana 47402-2682
www.worldwisdom.com

Contents

Editor's Preface   *vii*

Foreword   *xi*

Introduction to the Sacred Art of Christianity   1

The Role of Illuminated Manuscripts in Christian Art   5

    The Heavenly Jerusalem   26

The Foundations of Christian Art   37

    The Royal Portal of Chartres Cathedral   46

    Two Examples of Christian Symbolism   56

    The Portal of St. Gall   72

    Simone Martini   83

    The Theological Message of Russian Icons   89

The Decadence and the Renewal of Christian Art   91

    Late Renaissance and Baroque: "The Tragedy of Christian Art"   104

List of Illustrations   111

List of Sources   112

Index   113

Biographical Notes   115

Editor's Preface

Titus Burckhardt, the late Swiss art historian and cultural anthropologist, was one of the twentieth century's greatest experts on the sacred forms of the traditional civilizations that surrounded each of the world's great religions. This book brings together a collection of Burckhardt's articles on Christian sacred art from diverse sources, with page after page of illustrations from throughout the history of Christianity. These illustrations add life to his insightful descriptions and explanations, allowing the reader not only to understand, but also to taste, the beauty of the traditional Christian world that has for the most part passed into history.[1]

This book takes the reader on a historical journey that includes the emergence of Christian sacred art from Biblical manuscript illuminations. Burckhardt's articles trace the flowering of Christian sacred art and civilization over the following one and a half millennia, including architecture, iconography, and the arts and crafts guilds.

A characteristic of Burckhardt's scholarship is meticulous research into the writings of the chroniclers and outstanding personalities throughout the history of Christianity. He then includes extracts from these historical accounts that "allow contemporary witnesses to speak for themselves," thus providing an intimate glimpse into a past that is otherwise almost inaccessible.

The Foundations of Christian Art demonstrates that culture and spirituality are inextricably linked because each society's exterior culture is a social and artistic expression of its underlying religion. To illustrate this connection, Burckhardt points out that in the first one and a half millennia of Christianity virtually anyone making an object, including every member of a craft guild, was creating a work of art. During this time the terms "arts" and "crafts" were in some measure intertwined and art was the consequence of proper craftsmanship. It is hardly an exaggeration to say that every man was an artist.[2] As Burckhardt said, "No art merits that epithet

---

[1] The line drawings and diagrams in this book were either prepared or selected by Burckhardt. The illustrations are intended to represent some of the different styles and aesthetic ideas mentioned by the author, and are not meant as a comprehensive survey of Christian art.

[2] This idea is explored in detail in the anthology entitled *Every Man An Artist*, edited by Brian Keeble, World Wisdom, 2005.

[sacred art] unless its forms themselves reflect the spiritual vision characteristic of a particular religion."

The connotation of the term "art" began to change when the humanistic influences that emerged in the Renaissance no longer reflected the spiritual genius of Christianity. For the first time art began to refer to a select category of things that were only made by people who had a special aesthetic gift for creativity, based upon their own personal genius. As these artistic virtuosos competed to express their individual creativity in more innovative ways, their "art" became disconnected from any of the underlying spiritual principles that characterized Christian art in the previous one and a half millennia. The humanism of the Renaissance gave way to successive schools of art that eventually led to the "modernism" of the twentieth century, in which there are no objective criteria either for the style or the subject matter of art. The beauty that resulted when Christianity permeated almost every form of the Western medieval world is a direct contrast to the often ugly and fractured aesthetics of modern society that pervade our increasingly secular and individualistic world. It is therefore not surprising today that "art is in the eye of the beholder"; that people with highly charismatic personalities—even if they are mentally ill—are celebrated as great artists;[3] and that the most ugly or profane objects can be the subject of great art.

Despite his accurate portrayal of the decadence of the modern circumstance, Burckhardt still held out hope for a revitalization of Christian sacred art. The last chapter in this book, "The Decadence and the Renewal of Christian Art," presents the criteria for a rebirth of Christian art in the true sense of the term.

+ + +

The chapter entitled "The Role of Illuminated Manuscripts in Christian Art" is not to be found in any of Burckhardt's other books and has its own interesting history. It was written in the 1960s as a result of Burckhardt's pioneering research as the editor of several exquisite reproductions of illuminated medieval manuscripts, including the Book of Kells, the Book of Durrow, and the Book of Lindisfarne. The series of reproductions received wide acclaim and this article served as their companion piece in order to explain the importance of these early Christian manuscripts within the history of Christian art. The production of the Book of

---

[3] An excellent analysis of this consideration, including the exploration of what constitutes true "genius," can be found in Frithjof Schuon's article, "To Have a Center," which has been published both in Schuon's *To Have a Center*, World Wisdom, 1990, and in *Every Branch in Me: Essays on the Meaning of Man*, edited by Barry McDonald, World Wisdom, 2002.

Kells led to a lengthy personal audience with Pope Pius XII, which included a discussion of the so-called "Dark Ages" and the illustrated manuscripts that were so exquisitely produced during that time. At the end of the interview the Pope said to Burckhardt: "From the bottom of my heart I bless you, your family, your colleagues, and your friends."

+ + +

Burckhardt wrote two other books that focus on the Christian tradition. In the first, *Siena, City of the Virgin*, he "depict[s] the destiny of a town in which the spiritual development of the Christian Western world from the Middle Ages up to the present day is exemplified…." This book demonstrates that the city of Siena remains to this day one of the best preserved examples of a traditional Christian city. It also provides insights into the initial foundation of the city upon a sacred tradition and the subsequent decline of the city's sacred culture with the intrusion of later increasingly secular and humanistic values.

Burckhardt's master work on Christian sacred architecture can best be described in his own words: "The purpose of [*Chartres and the Birth of the Cathedral*] is to evoke as authentically as possible the spiritual climate in which the Gothic cathedral was born…. My aim is to show how the Gothic cathedral was the final fruit to ripen on the tree of an ancient tradition."

The Foundations of Christian Art is therefore a complement to Burckhardt's other two books on Christian art and civilization, *Siena* and *Chartres*. Together these three books demonstrate Burckhardt's unique ability to communicate the essence of the sacred Christian world as if we had lived during those times.

+ + +

Burckhardt's genius for understanding and interpreting sacred arts and crafts was not limited to Christianity. His seminal work, *Sacred Art in East and West*, deals with the artistic, cultural, and philosophical aspects of the Christian, Islamic, Buddhist, Hindu, and Far Eastern traditions. As William Stoddart has remarked in his editor's preface to *The Essential Titus Burckhardt*: "One of the things that strikes one most forcibly about Titus Burckhardt is the vastness of his range of interests. The world was indeed his parish."

Michael Oren Fitzgerald
March 2005
Bloomington, Indiana

PRIN CIPIO

ERAT UERBŪ

Foreword

Titus Burckhardt is an exponent of the permanent, the timeless; a domain which makes the use of the word "historian" redundant in a modern context. Burckhardt has done more than any other single author in the past 50, if not 100, years to recover the essential principles of the purpose of the arts—that is, if you accept the premise that the arts are more than mere hedonism and "individual expression."

Burckhardt, like the other few rare visionaries of this century, set about to get to the very roots of the arts of mankind. In doing so he recovered the deeper understanding that there is a detectable (albeit esoteric) universalism underlying those arts that genuinely reflect their civilization—not only reflect their respective civilizations, but have in fact *sustained* them by the very fact of constantly renewing the perennial truths that each civilization was founded upon.

His breadth and depth of scholarship is awe-inspiring: from the Classical world of Plato and the Pythagoreans, to Boethius and Cicero; from Aristotle to the School of Chartres. His knowledge of the Muslim poets, sages, scientists, musicians, and artists is equally broad and deep.

Art, he implies, represents a "timeless moment," an *is*-ness if such a phrase be allowable. We understand the older English when we say "thou *art*," meaning the permanence underlying the very essence of a person. Art, Burckhardt reveals, is exactly this direct reference to the permanent values in each culture and human society. Art, for Burckhardt, is at its best in revealing permanent truths; at its worst it is a betrayal of humanity in worldly hedonism and nihilism.

Due to his intrinsically spiritual nature, Burckhardt has revealed insight after insight into Christian symbolism and craft practice. Also, due to his turning to Sufism in the most committed and faithful manner, he revealed equally esoteric symbolic and hidden meanings in Islamic art.

The clarity with which the reader is taken simultaneously through the worlds of actuality,[1] symbolism, cultural specificity, and spiritual meaning, is the great achievement of this giant of the twentieth century. That he is yet to be properly known by a larger readership is not surprising—but inevitable given the world we inhabit today. This is due to the massive distractions and misleading paths of our own times. Yet there is a clearly visible yearning in the modern world for Truth, Goodness, and an unveiling of true Beauty, which Titus Burckhardt achieved. He will emerge in due time as one of the most important writers on the recovery of the true value of art in the twentieth century and even in the twenty-first century.

Keith Critchlow
September 2005

---

[1] Actuality is here used in contrast to Reality: "Reality" is the domain of the permanent; "actuality" is the ephemeral display we call "our world."

Introduction to the Sacred Art of Christianity

When historians of art apply the term "sacred art" to any and every work that has a religious subject, they are forgetting that art is essentially form. An art cannot properly be called "sacred" solely on the grounds that its subjects originate in a spiritual truth; its formal language also must bear witness to a similar origin. Such is by no means the case with a religious art like that of the Renaissance or of the Baroque period, which is in no way distinct, so far as style is concerned, from the fundamentally profane art of that era; neither the subjects which it borrows, in a wholly exterior and as it were literary manner, from religion, nor the devotional feelings with which it is permeated in appropriate cases, nor even the nobility of soul which sometimes finds expression in it, suffice to confer on it a sacred character. No art merits that epithet unless its forms themselves reflect the spiritual vision characteristic of a particular religion.

Every form is the vehicle of a given quality of being. The religious subject of a work of art may be as it were superimposed, it may have no relation to the formal "language" of the work, as is demonstrated by Christian art since the Renaissance; there are therefore essentially profane works of art with a sacred theme, but on the other hand there exists no sacred work of art which is profane in form, for there is a rigorous analogy between form and spirit. A spiritual vision necessarily finds its expression in a particular formal language; if that language is lacking, with the result that a so-called sacred art borrows its forms from some kind of profane art, then it can only be because a spiritual vision of things is also lacking.

It is useless to try to excuse the Protean style of a religious art, or its indefinite and ill-defined character, on grounds of the universality of dogma or the freedom of the spirit. Granted that spirituality in itself is independent of forms, this in no way implies that it can be expressed and transmitted by any and every sort of form. Through its qualitative essence form has a place in the sensible order analogous to that of truth in the intellectual order; this is the significance of the Greek notion of *eidos*. Just as a mental form such as a dogma or a doctrine can be the adequate, albeit limited, reflection of a Divine Truth, so can a sensible form retrace a truth or a reality which transcends both the plane of sensible forms and the plane of thought.

Every sacred art is therefore founded on a science of forms, or in other words, on the symbolism inherent in forms. It must be borne in mind that a symbol is not merely a conventional sign. It manifests its archetype by virtue of a definite onto-logical law; as Coomaraswamy has observed, a symbol *is* in a certain sense that to which it gives expression. For this very reason traditional symbolism is never with-out beauty: according to the spiritual view of the world, the beauty of an object is

Opposite: Altar fresco from the hermitage of Esquius, Catalonia, second half of the 12th century

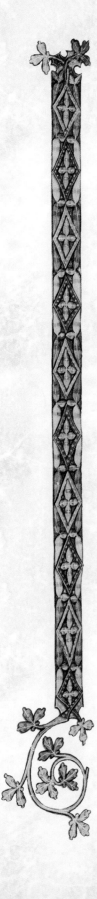

nothing but the transparency of its existential envelopes; an art worthy of the name is beautiful because it is true.

It is neither possible nor even useful that every artist or craftsman engaged in sacred art should be conscious of the Divine Law inherent in forms; he will know only certain aspects of it, or certain applications that arise within the limits of the rules of his craft; these rules will enable him to paint an icon, to fashion a sacred vessel, or to practice calligraphy in a liturgically valid manner, without its being necessary for him to know the ultimate significance of the symbols he is working with. It is tradition that transmits the sacred models and the working rules, and thereby guarantees the spiritual validity of the forms. Tradition has within itself a secret force which is communicated to an entire civilization and determines even arts and crafts the immediate objects of which include nothing particularly sacred. This force creates the style of a traditional civilization; a style that could never be imitated from outside is perpetuated without difficulty, in a quasi-organic manner, by the power of the spirit that animates it and by nothing else.

One of the most tenacious of typically modern prejudices is the one that sets itself up against the impersonal and objective rules of an art, for fear that they should stifle creative genius. In reality no work exists that is traditional, and there-fore "bound" by changeless principles, which does not give sensible expression to a certain creative joy of the soul; whereas modern individualism has produced, apart from a few works of genius which are nevertheless spiritually barren, all the ugliness—the endless and despairing ugliness—of the forms which permeate the "ordinary life" of our times.

One of the fundamental conditions of happiness is to know that everything that one does has a meaning in eternity; but who in these days can still conceive of a civilization within which all vital manifestations would be developed "in the likeness of Heaven"?[1]

From the Christian point of view God is "artist" in the most exalted sense of the word, because He created man "in His own image" (Genesis 1:27). And moreover since the image comprises not only a likeness to its model, but also a quasi-absolute unlikeness, it could not but become corrupted. The divine reflection in man was troubled by the fall of Adam; the mirror was tarnished; but neverthe-less man could not be completely cast aside; for while the creature is subject to its own limitations, the Divine Plenitude on the other hand is not subject to limitation of any kind, and this amounts to saying that the said limitations cannot be in any real sense opposed to the Divine Plenitude, which is manifested as limitless Love. The very limitlessness of that Love demands that God, "pronouncing" Himself as Eternal Word, should descend into this world, and as it were assume the perishable outlines of the image—human nature—so as to restore to it its original beauty.

In Christianity the divine image *par excellence* is the human form of the Christ; thus it comes about that Christian art has but one purpose: the transfigura-tion of man, and of the world which depends on man, by their participation in the Christ.

---

[1] "Do you not know, O Asclepius, that Egypt is the image of Heaven and that it is the projection here below of the whole ordering of heavenly things?" (*Hermes Trismegistus,* from the French translation of L. Ménard).

The Christ-Logos as Creator, with Sophia, miniature from Flavius Josephus' *Antiquitates iudaici*, late 12th century

The Role of Illuminated Manuscripts in Christian Art

Shortly after the Second World War I visited the small Chapter library of Verona Cathedral. The building itself in the old city had suffered much by bombing; its severe Romanesque inner cloister was still full of rubble, but the collection of manuscripts and incunabula had been saved and was housed temporarily in one of the rooms overlooking the river Adige. The librarian, a pale and sensitive young priest, showed me one famous volume after another: the *Commentarii institutionum* of Gaius, the only surviving handbook of pre-Christian Roman law, the *Pandectae* of Justinian, a very early Euclid and an equally early Virgil, the *Didascalia Apostolorum*, the oldest text of the Mass dating back to the second century, the *Sacramentarium Leonianum* of the sixth and the *Breviarium Mozarabicum* of the eighth century, together with a Gospel book of the fifth century written in silver and gold on purple stained vellum. Finally he produced a large, heavy manuscript of the fifth century, an almost complete example of St. Augustine's *City of God*. "Imagine it, this book was probably written in the lifetime of St. Augustine himself, he may even have held this very book in his hands!" As he said this his own hands began to tremble with reverence.

Here, faced by these manuscripts one could feel something of what the book must have meant in the early years of the Christian West. The few books that had survived the onslaught of the barbarian invasions, with which an abbot would have been able to endow a new monastery or a bishop a new church, and which were then copied again and again, were at the same time the spiritual and intellectual seeds which were to lead to all later harvests. Some transmitted the fundamental premises of Roman and Greek knowledge, others passed down the teaching of the Fathers of the Church, while the most precious of all contained the very words of God's message to mankind. These were subject to the richest decoration, as was the choir of a church which enshrined all that is most holy. On these was lavished the finest creative ability of the time. One enclosed them in silver coffers, decorated their covers with gold, ivory, and gems and painted their pages with ornaments and miniatures.

Because such a book could be taken from place to place, more so almost than any other kind of work of art, it served as a model for artistic creation, especially in areas where indigenous artists had not hitherto been able to see the like. Frequently miniatures from a manuscript served as models for a cycle of wall-paintings or even sculptures in relief. If the book came from a distant land, or if it was the work of the founder of a monastery, one saw in it the witness of tradition. Just as the text was given word for word, so the pictures belonging to it were carefully copied. In this

Initial from *Priscian's Grammar*, St. Gall

way book illuminations can be traced like a silver thread running through the first millennium of Christian art.

For us, surviving early medieval manuscripts are often the only reliable witnesses of whole epochs and of cultural regions from which other work has hardly been passed down to us at all, in an unchanged form. Most of the buildings of the early Middle Ages were either destroyed or altered in later times; wall-paintings have disintegrated or have faded beyond recognition, and work in precious metals was, with very few exceptions, melted down in periods of need or of ignorance. Syria is said to be the birthplace of early Christian painting, but only very few illuminated manuscripts bear witness to what her early pictorial art looked like. The same is true of early Christian Ireland and England whose surprising formal inventions could hardly be imagined but for the few extant illuminated manuscripts. Some of these manuscripts appear to our eyes to be something of a miracle—being today still as fresh as the day on which they were written and decorated. Even when they bear the traces of constant use, like the smoke of candles having blackened pages exhibited to the faithful on holy days, or when the humid atmosphere of the nearby sea has disfigured the surface of the vellum here and there, the colors retain much of their original brilliance and the hand of the man who once created their pages still bridges the gap of centuries. Only an interior, unaltered in its structure and in all its fittings, can make a similar impression of immediacy on us.

The experience of such an interior cannot be held fast by us—no reproduction can retain it convincingly. With a manuscript, however, matters are different. With the technical means that are today at our disposal its impact can be reproduced, if not wholly, at least with a great degree of accuracy. This presents us with a task which appears all the more urgent in view of the fact that the recent war has proved to us how easily a library can be destroyed. The most truthful possible reproduction of a manuscript fulfills the need to make such precious codices available to all—codices which are normally only accessible to the very few privileged among us, who study them and who are allowed to turn their pages. In a facsimile—and that is its special charm—one owns, in a way, the original itself, and in the same size in which it was designed to be seen.

The Book of Kells

To edit the famous Book of Kells in facsimile was the first task that presented itself to us. The manuscript is a Latin Gospel book of the eighth century, which probably originated in Iona, a lonely island off the West coast of Scotland, then inhabited by Irish monks, and which was probably taken to Kells in central Ireland, by a later abbot who fled from the invading Vikings. After the suppression of the monasteries by Henry VIII of England, it passed into the possession of Trinity College, Dublin, where it is preserved as the greatest national treasure. It is indeed a hidden treasure hoard that has survived the centuries. The splendor and elegance of its decoration, people once believed, was the work of an angel. Geraldus Cambrensis, who visited Kildare in 1185, described a book, which could hardly have been any other than the Book of Kells, in the following terms: "Of all the marvels of Kildare, I recall noth-

Opposite: *The Monogram Page*, the Book of Kells, folio 34r

generatio

diligenter donec inueniat & cum inuene
rit conuocat amicos & uicinos dicens
congratulamini mihi quia inueni drag
mam quam perdideram

dico uobis gaudium erit coram
angelis di super uno peccatore
pęnitentiam agente

aitautem homo quidam habuit
duos filios & dixit adulescen
tior ex illis patri pater da mihi
portionem substantiae quae
me contingit & diuisit illis substan
tiam & non post multos dies congre
gatis omnib: adulescentior filius
peregre profectus est in regionem

ing more marvelous than that wonderful book, written, they say, at the dictation of an angel in the days of St. Brigid. This book contains the harmony of the four evangelists according to Jerome, where for almost every page there are different designs, distinguished by varied colors. Here you may see the face of majesty, divinely drawn, here the mystic symbols of the evangelists, each with wings, now six, now four, now two; here the eagle, there the calf, here the man, and there the lion, and other forms almost infinite. Look at them superficially with the ordinary casual glance, and you would think it an erasure, and not tracery. Fine craftsmanship is all about you, but you might not notice it. Look more keenly at it, and you will penetrate to the very shrine of art. You will make out intricacies, so delicate and subtle, so exact and compact, so full of knots and links, with colors so fresh and vivid, that you might say that all this was the work of an angel, and not of a man. For my part the oftener I see the book, and the more carefully I study it, the more I am lost in ever fresh amazement, and I see more and more wonders in the book."

Decorative detail from the Book of Kells

Still today, anyone who looks at the decorative pages at the beginning of each of the Gospels will be astonished by the unbelievably fine and exact net of geometric pattern that fills them. No less great is the art of calligraphy which in its balanced forms and never flagging rhythm runs clear and pure for the six hundred pages of the book.

Irish Script

Irish monks were unsurpassed masters of calligraphy. One may say that they solved the problem of turning the static letters of the Romans, more suited to engraving in stone, into a flowing rhythm without losing their clear differentiation of forms. Irish script exerted a strong influence on the art of writing on the Continent; its influence can be traced in the Carolingian minuscule, and in fact can still be found in the humanist scripts of the Renaissance, although the influence of classicism and the effect of printing then allowed the lines of script to become brittle and unrhythmical again. Irish monks were also the first to develop the opening letters of a text into a decorative feature. The illuminated initial, the main element of Western book decoration, is derived from them. The geometric forms of the letter struck a chord in the Irish that touched their feeling for the similar geometric motifs in their indigenous Celtic art.

So, quite spontaneously they saw in the individual letter an ornament, and not only an ornament, because these geometric signs had to have a kind of sacramental significance for them, or they could not have used them to honor the word of God.

Early Christian Culture in Ireland

The spiritual individuality of the Irish monks may be explained by the fact that Christianity in Ireland did not expand, as it did in nearly all other countries, on a basis of Roman colonization. The Romans had never occupied Ireland; here the Church did not settle into the groove of an existing Roman administration, nor had the spiritual life to adjust itself to a way of thought which Rome had created. Pre-Christian Irish culture was purely Celtic but its form was such that it was able to accept Christian teaching without any great inner revolution and almost without putting up any fight. Although ancient Irish culture may be considered "barbaric" according to Roman or even modern ideas, because it shunned urban and technical development, yet it had the advantage of an organically organized society, whose upper levels were concerned with the preservation of traditional knowledge. To this intellectual elite, the *aes dána*, belonged not only priests and scientists, but also poets, doctors, and the masters of the fine arts. As Christianity spread in Ireland in the fifth century, it first conquered these upper layers of society and this explains why the forms of ancient Irish art were transferred without a break to a liturgical function in the Church.

Cross on folio 85v of the Durrow Gospels

At a time when the migration of peoples spread destruction on the Continent, a Christian culture flourished undisturbed in Ireland, a culture which later, as the flood of the migration was turned, sowed the seed of the spiritual life in central Europe. With Christian Rome, Ireland had up to then only had tenuous connections, but along the sea routes she had maintained close bonds with the Christian East. The spiritual life in Ireland was controlled by the monasteries. The abbots had the power, and even the bishops were under their jurisdiction, perhaps because there were no proper cities. So the early medieval culture of Ireland was at the same time highly developed and primitive, not unlike the culture which existed until recently in Tibet. Around the monasteries, in which the sciences and the arts were cultivated, lived the population in half-nomadic circumstances. And the Irish shepherd as well as the monk or the hermit retained that kind of inner communion with nature which can so easily be the setting of the contemplative life:

> I have a bothy in the wood
> none knows it save the Lord, my God;
> one wall an ash, the other hazel,
> and a great fern makes the door.
>
> The doorposts are made of heather,
> the lintel of honeysuckle;
> and wild forest all around
> yields mast for well-fed swine.
>
> This size my hut: the smallest thing,
> homestead amid well-trod paths;
> a woman (but blackbird clothed and seeming)
> warbles sweetly from its gable.

The Book of Durrow

At the beginning of Irish book illumination is found another work, also in the library of Trinity College, which in spite of its simpler style—or just because of it—is not inferior in beauty to the more famous Book of Kells. That is the so-called

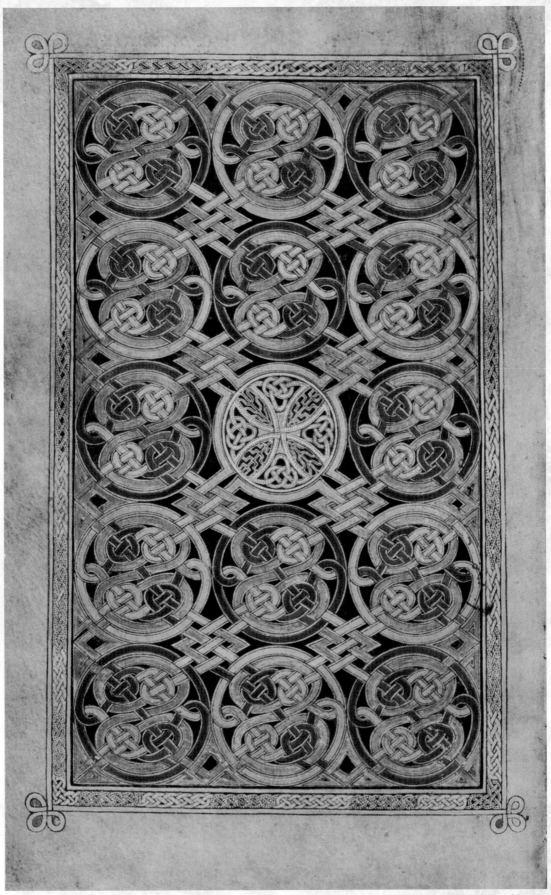

Carpet Page, the Book of Durrow, folio 85v

The Beginning of the Gospel according to St. John, the Book of Durrow, folio 193r

Book of Durrow, the oldest illuminated manuscript of insular origin that survives in a complete form. In contrast to the uncontrolled splendor of the Book of Kells, the decorative pages of this older work, a Gospel book of the seventh century, emanate a serene calm. One has characterized these miniatures as "primitive," but they are not. It is true, one can still see ancient Celtic spirals and Germanic animal ornament introduced from the East, as separate entities in it. The geometric structure, however, which is created out of these disparate elements has a convincing sense of unity. Perhaps one may not see this unity at first sight, because the interpenetration of spirals, and of the magic interlace of ribbons, or of unending chains of animals fighting themselves and others, draw the eye along their own continuous movement. But this movement remains, like the waves that form under the arches of a bridge, controlled by an all-pervading law of calm; the more one penetrates into its movement, the more the higher unity becomes apparent—a unity formed in masterly fashion from opposing tensions, never empty or tired.

The normal pages of the text of the Book of Durrow are hardly ornamented at all, bearing only simple initials, but the beginnings of each of the four Gospels is emphasized by several highly ornamented pages. First a page with the symbol of the Evangelist, then a so-called "carpet" page, on which the interlaced pattern usually includes the motif of a cross, followed by the opening words of the text, enlarged into great and mysterious signs. Three colors, a golden yellow, brick red, and a muted green interact in a hundred degrees of intensity—the task of reproducing them was far from easy.

From the period between the Durrow Gospels, the earliest of the Hiberno-Saxon illuminated books, and the Book of Kells, which represents the latest peak in insular illumination before it came to terms with Continental work, a number of codices have survived of a high artistic standard. The largest and most beautiful among them is the Gospel book of Lindisfarne, written about the year 700 and now preserved in the British Museum.

The Early Northumbrian Manuscripts

Lindisfarne is a small island off the coast of Northumbria. Irish monks had founded a monastery there. They acted as missionaries in their Anglo-Saxon surroundings, and out of the combination of Irish and Anglo-Saxon motifs a special style was developed that is called Northumbrian. It appears in a number of other Northumbrian manuscripts, as well as in the Lindisfarne Gospels. To this group belong the noble, but heavily damaged Gospels of St. Chad in the cathedral library of Lichfield, a Gospel book in the cathedral of Durham, and the Echternach Gospels, now in the Bibliothèque Nationale in Paris.

The monastery of Echternach in Luxembourg was an Irish foundation like many other early monasteries, from the north of France down to the Alps, and even as far south as Naples and Taranto. At all these places, the Irish monks must have left manuscripts behind them, but only a few of them have survived. One of the most important collections of early Irish miniatures is to be found in the Abbey Library of St. Gall in Switzerland. Gallus, a follower of that active missionary, the Abbot Columbanus, settled as a hermit in the valley of the Steinach. His own followers were Alemanns, but the monastery which they built also attracted other wandering Irish monks, who no doubt occasionally brought their own books with them. Most of them have disappeared over the centuries, except for one Gospel book with most impressive miniatures, the so-called Codex 51, a copy of the grammatical treatise of Priscian illustrated with pen drawings, and a number of fragments which in part were discovered in the bindings of later manuscripts.

The reproduction of the Irish miniatures of St. Gall was

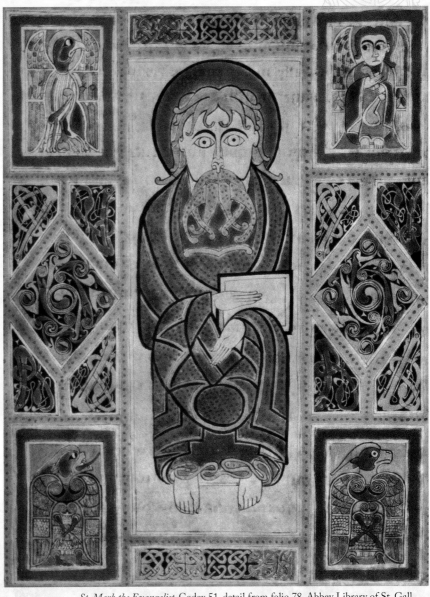

St. Mark the Evangelist, Codex 51, detail from folio 78, Abbey Library of St. Gall

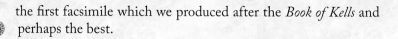

the first facsimile which we produced after the *Book of Kells* and perhaps the best.

The Lindisfarne Gospels

As I approached the Director of the British Museum, then Sir Thomas Kendrick, and asked him for permission to reproduce the Lindisfarne Gospels, he allowed me to proceed on the understanding that the facsimile would be produced by the same technicians that had been responsible for editions of the Book of Kells and the Irish miniatures of St. Gall. "You must realize," he said to me, "that in the Lindisfarne Gospels you are dealing with a Codex that is artistically far superior to the Book of Kells." I was reminded of our Irish friends in Dublin who had spoken, in a somewhat derogatory manner, of the "stiff Anglo-Saxon book from Lindisfarne, that cannot stand comparison with a genuinely Irish work." In fact, the Book of Kells represents the overabundant splendor of a tree which was to bear no more fruit; it is more imaginative than the Lindisfarne Codex which is some eighty years earlier in date, but the latter shows a stricter artistic discipline, perhaps because it is still related to the indigenous goldsmith's work, dominated by the compass and the graver. The precious "carpet-pages" with which each Gospel opens, undoubtedly had splendid and carefully executed pieces of goldsmith's work inlaid with glass or precious stones for their models. Proof of this can be found in the British Museum, since the treasure of the Sutton-Hoo ship-burial, found just before the war, has been on exhibition there. This treasure demonstrates clearly the kind of precious material that was available during the seventh century at the court of an Anglo-Saxon chieftain. Alongside the great Irish hanging-bowls, decorated with enameled escutcheons, in one of which a bronze fish appears to swim—one does not know what purpose these bowls served—there are Byzantine silver dishes, a shield decorated with gilt-bronze plaques and an iron boss, a sword with golden pommel, gold buckles, and other jewelry, their surfaces covered with garnets and millefiori glass. The Keeper of British and Medieval Antiquities[1] led me to one of the cases, unlocked it, and handed me a decorative stud from the sheath of a sword, no larger than a thimble and formed like a truncated pyramid, inlaid with more than sixty garnets. "One of the best jewelers in London assures me," he remarked, "that a goldsmith, with all the modern equipment at his command, would have to work for many days to cut only one of these corner stones." The Keeper of British and Medieval Antiquities, who wrote the archaeological commentary for the edition of the manuscript, was to discover among other things the precise net of lines and circles drawn on the vellum, with which the illuminator set out his decoration of spirals and interlaced animals before painting them on to the page. Strangely enough, the painter hardly ever used gold as one of his colors. And yet the decorative pages are as luminous and sparkling as if they were made of the most precious materials. They have totally preserved their freshness to this day.

[1] Mr. R.L.S. Bruce-Mitford.

Opposite: Cross-Carpet Page Introducing the Gospel according to St. John, the Lindisfarne Gospels, folio 210b

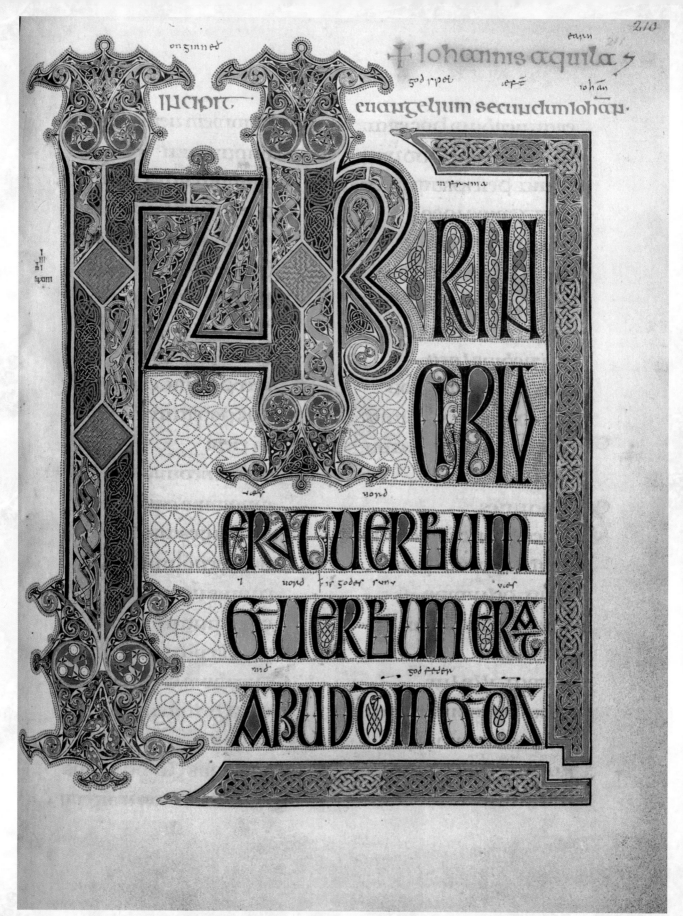

Major Decorated Initial at the Beginning of the Gospel according to St. John, the Lindisfarne Gospels, folio 211

The Scriptorium of Lindisfarne

The illuminator—it was to be discovered that one man wrote and illuminated the whole book single-handed—was called Eadfrith, later Bishop of Lindisfarne. An art of painting and writing as considerable as that of Eadfrith, of necessity created a school. Our Gospel book cannot have been the only one produced by the scriptorium of Lindisfarne. The research into this problem was taken over by a scholar, Julian T. Brown.[2] He was to discover that at least three more manuscripts came from the same scriptorium, namely Ms. 92 of Lincoln College, Oxford, the Durham Gospels, and the great Echternach Gospels in Paris, calligraphically so superb.

But the Lindisfarne Gospels was yet to yield more information. Between the lines of the Latin text of the Gospels, which is related to the Vulgate, a full translation was added in the tenth century in the vernacular, which puts on record the precise moment when the Anglo-Saxon language branched off from other North-Germanic dialects. These interlinear "glosses" were discussed by Alan S.C. Ross of Birmingham, a scholar who had first been an astronomer and who then changed over to Germanic philology. He worked with "astronomical" precision, and a glossary of this text running into many thousand entries, adds up to a veritable dictionary of the Anglo-Saxon language. This was to form a part of our scholarly commentary on the manuscript.

Initial from *Priscian's Grammar* in St. Gall

Even that was not all. The colors which Eadfrith had used were to be examined scientifically. Because one could not scrape off even the minutest particles, it had to be done with the aid of spectrum analysis. Dr. A.E.A. Werner, Keeper of the Research Laboratory of the British Museum, undertook this task. Later Dr. H. Rosen-Runge joined him, introducing a new and unexpected method. Certain recipes, which have been preserved in early medieval workshop texts had long been known, but had been considered only superstitious, because they listed such strange materials. But now the German scholar took these recipes at their word and spared no effort to assemble the odd substances described, be they a kind of aphis from Sicily, which had to be specially bred, a kind of shellfish to be fished out of the North Sea, or be it that copper-filings had to be brewed together with all sorts of herbs in a hollow tree-trunk. And lo and behold, these experiments gave us precisely those colors with which medieval illuminations were painted. Dr. Rosen-Runge manufactured those very colors, with which Eadfrith might have painted, and comparing his results microscopically with those in our Gospels, confirmed the accuracy of his premises.

The Meaning of Early Christian Decorative Forms

When faced by the decorated pages of the Lindisfarne Gospels, woven out of hundreds of motifs, one may ask oneself what these forms meant to the monks themselves who painted them. Although we have no precise evidence, there can be no doubt that those things, which appear to us today as ornament, were then, in a period still half-archaic, not the result simply of aesthetic playfulness. Ornament,

---

[2] He was later a Professor of Palaeography at King's College, London.

which is nothing but decoration and means no more than that, only really exists in a period when all meaningful content of art is expressed in naturalistic terms. Pure ornament is then retained as a kind of frame only—the last refuge of a non-naturalistic play of forms. For an "archaic" culture—still in really close contact with nature—every form, however "abstract" it may be, has right from the start a name and a meaning. Space and time are not considered as separate from each other, and for that reason nature is not represented, but symbols are created which express cosmic events totally, and in terms of eternity. So the circle is both a picture of the path of the sun and of time. The equal armed cross inscribed in it, divides space not only into North, South, East, and West, but divides time also into the parts of the day and the four seasons of the year. A double spiral indicates the rhythm of the sun's orbit, because in the change from the summer to the winter path and vice versa it seems to move in increasing or decreasing circles, as if the sun "unwraps" itself and again "wraps" itself up. In this, the rhythm of coming into being and passing away itself seems to be expressed. If one links double spirals to one another in the form of a chain—a "meander"—one creates thereby a picture of continuous cosmic events.

The best evidence for the fact that the geometric motifs of insular art still had a more or less clearly understood meaning for the Irish scribe, is that he combined them with letter forms to create those mysterious, great initials which decorate the opening pages of the Gospels like seals, only to be opened by the initiated. For the monks of the seventh and eighth centuries these words meant more than just the start of a story—they were "words of life."

Another indication that for the illuminator of the Lindisfarne Gospels these forms, which appear to us to be only ornament, enshrined a reality greater than a naturalistic representation, lies in the fact that he remained true to these forms even when he knew models of Hellenistic style perfectly well. Only about fifty miles away the so-called Codex Amiatinus was being copied from a Mediterranean prototype probably imported from Naples, in the monastery of Wearmouth founded under the influence of Rome. This large and heavy codex was intended as a present for the pope. However, it never got as far as Rome because the cleric, who transported it on the back of a mule over the Alps, died on the way on Monte Amiata, and today the codex is preserved in the Laurentian Library in Florence. It contains a representation of the Prophet Ezra, writing, painted with all the late Hellenistic pictorial skill, with its foreshortened forms, its shadows, and its highlights, in short, with the illusion of three dimensional space which is otherwise totally unknown in early Insular book illumination. Eadfrith had known the prototype from Naples, because it is distantly reflected in his representation of the Apostle Matthew. He certainly knew Greek-Byzantine models, as is proved by the general composition of his Evangelist portraits and especially by their inscriptions: "Hagios Lucas," "Hagios Johannes" and so on. And in spite of that, he remained faithful to the rules of his art, based entirely on line and flat color. Clearly, for him more truth to reality was contained in the geometric spirals, the interlaced bands, and the stylized animals which appear in pairs, or struggle against each other. This is Nature, not as she appears externally, but how her inner life is created by a play of opposing and mutually compensating forces. These forces appear to follow irra-

tional impulses, and yet, seen on the whole, obey an unchangeable law; the "Natura domitata," tamed nature, who, in spite of her gruesome and yet beautiful game, has to serve God's eternal command.

Surely the same concept can be found in an early Irish hymn, attributed to St. Patrick, a hymn which has been called the "Deer's Cry" because, due to its magic power, the Saint and his companions appeared as a herd of deer in the eyes of enemies lying in wait for them. After the Trinity, the Choir of Angels, the Patriarchs, the Prophets, and the Saints, the powers of Nature are called upon:

> I rise today
> by the power of Heaven,
> by the power of the sun's light,
> the moon's brightness,
> the fire's gleaming,
> the lightning's quickness,
> the wind's roaring, the sea's depth,
> the earth's firmness,
> and the rocks' hardness….

Because all is one and the same God ordained unity.

The Ambrosian Iliad

The opposite pole to Irish ornament, and the other root of medieval book illumination, is figurative illustration as it was known among the pagan Greeks and Romans. One of the purest examples of this art to have survived is the manuscript of

Miniature XLVI, the Ambrosian Iliad, c. 5th century

Detail of a miniature from the Codex Pupureus of Rossano depicting the parable of the wise and foolish virgins

Homer's Iliad, which is preserved in the Ambrosian Library in Milan. This manuscript, probably produced in the fifth century, exemplifies the link between the classical book illustration of the Greeks with that of the Christian Middle Ages. It is the only example of the pagan-Greek art of the book to survive: nearly all early illuminated manuscripts are religious texts.

The Iliad of the Ambrosian Library is the earliest illustrated book of secular content and at the same time the last extant witness of a school of artists who looked back to a rich heritage. After all, the Iliad was one of the most widely read books in the Greco-Roman world and its illustration must have been able to draw on hundreds of sources. The Milan manuscript was originally a whole book, but at some time a collector cut the miniatures out of their pages—and they alone survive, as fifty-two loose pages, together with those parts of the Greek text which are found on the back of the paintings.

Classical Greek painting is here translated into a kind of cursive form which, with its nervous line and its suggestive coloring, has a somewhat decadent charm all of its own, while in its rhythmic grouping of armies, in the differentiation of scale for heroes and gods, and in the simplification of the ships lying at anchor, and the cities in the background, the Byzantine style is already suggested. The drama of the scenes, still bearing the mark of antique pathos, and yet betraying already a certain spiritual uneasiness, shows that pole of European culture to which the one found in the early Irish manuscripts and the Celtic heritage within them is the exact opposite. The love for the purely human, the turbulence and the effort of the will searching for new conquests, somehow already foreshadow the Renaissance.

The Late Antique Manuscripts

Most closely related to the Ambrosian Iliad are the so-called Itala Fragments of Quedlinburg which are preserved in the Staatsbibliothek of Berlin and the Vatican Virgil, an illustrated Aeneid in the Vatican Library. A second early Virgil manuscript in the Vatican, the so-called Vergilius Romanus with its scenes of the Georgica, is already remote from the Hellenistic heritage and naively imitating antique patterns.

The real center of gravity of Christian culture in the early Middle Ages was neither in Ireland nor in Rome, but in the East. Christian pictorial art is said to have begun in Syria, and in the wall-painting which decorated the churches at the birthplace and at the Tomb of our Lord, in the Holy Land itself, the forms were first created that were to be decisive for all the Christian world. These paintings, which represented the life of the Savior on earth, were believed to have been inspired by the Holy Ghost, and the fact that they inspired Christian art for centuries lends credence to this belief.

Early Christian Book Illumination in Syria

The early Christian wall-paintings in Syria and in Palestine have not survived. One would have expected to find their reflection in illuminated manuscripts, but nearly all of those were destroyed in the seventh and eighth centuries, when the iconoclast emperors of Byzantium ordered the destruction of all representation

of holy personages. Hardly more than four sixth century manuscripts of Syriac-Byzantine provenance decorated with miniatures have come down to us. Of those four, three form a group because they are all written and illuminated on purple-stained vellum. The Vienna Genesis, so called because it is now in the Nationalbibliothek in Vienna, the Sinope Gospels in the Bibliothéque Nationale in Paris, and the Codex Rossanensis, in the remote monastery of Rossano in Calabria. The most impressive of the three purple codices is that of Rossano. Against the wine-red background of its pages, which conjures up a mood of sublime intoxication, figures painted in tempera with highlights of blueish white and gold appear as if lit suddenly by shafts of moonlight. The wall-paintings of the Holy Places of the East, however, appear to be reflected only in the fourth manuscript, the so-called Rabbula Gospels. The monk Rabbula, who wrote the book in the monastery of St. John at Zagba in Mesopotamia, wrote down the date 586 together with his name. Perhaps only the fact that this desert monastery was, at the time of the beginning of iconoclasm, already cut off from the Byzantine Empire by the advancing Arab army, has enabled

The Virgin and Child under a Canopy, the Rabbula Gospels, folio Iv

this manuscript to survive. A few entries in Arabic prove that the book lived for a considerable time in the world of Islam. Although everything that has been written on Early Christian Art refers to this manuscript in Florence, its miniatures have until now never been published in full.

The first illuminated page—in reality the last, because Syriac writing is read from right to left—shows the Virgin and Child under a canopy, with two peacocks approaching from left and right above. This is one of the earliest surviving pictures of the *Theotokos* (Mother of God) in all her regal glory. The page opposite is filled by a double portrait of the Fathers Eusebius of Caesarea and Ammonius of Alexandria, and this is followed by nineteen pages with the Eusebian Canon tables, which are conceived as richly decorated portals surrounded by small scenes from the Old and the New Testament. The four last illuminated pages all show compositions which in their monumental structure remind one of wall-paintings. They represent the Crucifixion, the Resurrection with the Mary's at the Tomb, the Ascension, the Enthroned Christ, and Pentecost. But the other paintings are of finer quality and those small scenes scattered about the Canon tables have the greatest pictorial charm. In their content too, they are the most important. Christian typology—the revealing juxtapositioning of scenes from the Old and New Testaments, which was to dominate all of Western medieval art—is here already suggested. The Rabbula Gospels show clearly the confluence of artistic traditions, from which Christian art was to create a new synthesis. The Greco-Roman forms can still be recognized and at the same time one can sense the proximity of Persia and Egypt. The transformation by the Christian spirit is still incomplete, still groping and uncertain. One might almost say that the violent incursion of Byzantine iconoclasm became necessary so that Christian pictorial art could rise to a full awareness of its own formal language.

Mozarabic Book Illumination

The manuscripts so far described all belong to pre-Carolingian times, the early Middle Ages in its narrower sense. With the creation of the new Roman Empire by Charlemagne, a new epoch begins not least in book illumination. Its many contributaries flow together into a new stream, and suddenly there appears much similar work side by side and at much the same time. Also, book illumination self-consciously looks back to late-Antique models. But the boundaries of early medieval art cannot be drawn everywhere at exactly the same time. In Spain, separated as it was from central Europe by the rule of its Moorish courts, a branch of early Christian

Canon Table, Biblia Hispalense, folio 278r

book illumination, saturated by Moorish elements, continued to flourish well on into the ninth and tenth century. This was in no way an art of the "Ghetto," because the Spanish Christian community had preserved its full freedom of worship under their Moorish masters. The ecclesiastical constitution of the Visigothic Kingdom continued to function. The Archbishops of Toledo continued to rule over all Spanish sees. Monasteries and Christian schools functioned fully. And although the Christians under the rule of the Emir or Caliph of Córdoba were called by the Arabic name *must'arab*—"mozárabes," which means "made arabic," their liturgical language continued to be Latin. They even maintained bonds, albeit rather loose ones, with Rome. But because they were drawn into the Islamic cultural orbit, which linked Spain with North Africa, Egypt, Syria, and even Asia, they naturally looked to the East and were open to the influences from Christian centers that had existed there from the earliest days. Mozarabic painting seems to reflect oriental models far removed in space and time, not only those from Coptic Egypt and from Syria, but even Iranian, which Moorish decorative art no doubt transmitted to Spain. An influence of the ancient Orient difficult to define in detail overpowered the naturalism of the Greco-Roman heritage and created an archaic as well as timeless formal language which lends a magic power to its pictures.

Adoration of the Lamb, Beatus Apocalypse, Santo Domingo de Silos

Beatus of Liébana's Commentary to the Apocalypse

The most important group of ancient Spanish illuminated manuscripts is formed by 22 copies, some incomplete and variously illustrated, of a lost original, the Commentary to the Apocalypse by Beatus of Liébana. This book played an important part in the early history of Spain. Beatus of Liébana, a monk who lived in the eighth century in Asturias, a mountainous region of northern Spain never permanently conquered by the Moors, ran into a dispute over dogma with his spiritual superior, the Archbishop of Toledo. The archbishop, Elipandus, formulated the dogma of Christ's nature as the Son of God at a Council of Sevilla, in a way that Beatus considered a betrayal of Christian teaching. It may be that Elipandus wished to

meet the Islamic perspective half-way when, in his exposition of the doctrine of the Holy Trinity, he sought to make a distinction between the essential divine Sonship, identifiable with the eternal Word or Logos, and an "adoptive" Sonship, deemed to belong to Jesus as man, and shared with all the saints. The Koran in fact recognizes the spiritual derivation of Christ from God. It calls Him "Spirit of God and His Word, which He sent down on Mary," but it avoids the expression "Son of God" for the man Jesus on the ground that man, as a creature, cannot be of the same nature as his Creator. Islamic solicitude for the incomparability of God rules out such an expression as "Father and Son." Archbishop Elipandus perhaps wanted to answer the Islamic objection and at the same time to create a bridge between the two faiths. But with this explanation, despite his good intentions, he found himself in contradiction to the dogma of the unity of the Person in Christ. Within a given religious system all doctrines are related to one another as are the geometrical axes in the interior of a crystal. The transparency of the crystal, its "permeability" to the Divine Light, depends on this inner unity, which is a different one from crystal to crystal.

Beatus was therefore in the right when he cried "betrayal" and declared war on the Archbishop of Toledo. He won the support of Charlemagne who would have been pleased to extend his Christian Empire into Spain. The Councils of Rome, Regensburg, Frankfurt, and Aachen condemned the "adoptive" dogma of Elipandus. Charlemagne, who had entered Spain some six years earlier, did not at that time have much success against the Muslims because most Mozarabic Christians preferred their rule to that of the Franks. Now that the head of the Visigothic Church, recognized and protected by the Muslims, was a heretic, Spanish Christians could find salvation in only one way—revolt against their Muslim rulers. In this sense Beatus of Liébana, who is venerated as a saint in Asturias, became the spiritual ancestor of the "reconquista"—the reconquest of Spain by Latin Christianity.

Perhaps because this fight appeared to him to be a kind of overture to the trials and tribulations of the Last Judgment, or perhaps only because he wanted to prove the divinity of Christ, he wrote his great commentary on the Apocalypse, in which he explained each passage step by step by reference to the relevant evidence provided by the Fathers of the Church. He made use of patristic literature which has survived to this day and also

Christ in Majesty, Moralia In Iob of 945, folio 2

Opposite: *Christ the Victor*, Beatus of Liébana, folio 151

parts that have not survived and which we know only from his quotations. To the Apocalypse proper, he also added the Book of Daniel.

His work became widely known. One knew that the secret Revelation of St. John predicted the fate of man at the end of the world in symbolic form. No better explanations of the secret revealed in this book could be given than those provided by the Fathers of the Church who spoke through Beatus: In this book the key to the future was to be found.

The Heavenly Jerusalem

We reproduce here a miniature of the Heavenly Jerusalem taken from a manuscript of the eleventh century, the so-called Apocalypse of Saint-Séver which belongs to a certain group of medieval manuscripts, mostly of Spanish origin and all stemming from a single prototype, a commentary on the Apocalypse written by the Asturian monk Beatus de Liébana towards the end of the eighth century. The same image of the Heavenly Jerusalem occurs in most of these manuscripts, with only slight variations, so that one can admit that its composition goes back to the prototype, which is now lost.

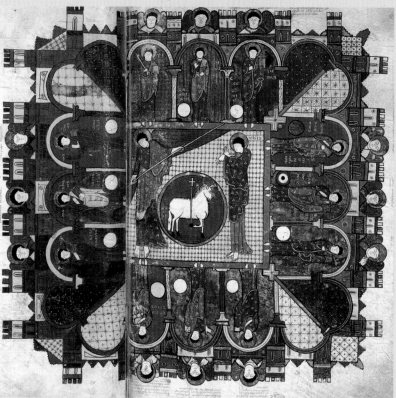

The artist made use of a kind of abstract perspective, familiar to medieval readers and viewers: he represented the heavenly city as if seen from above, with its walls projected onto the horizontal plane. In this way, he could portray the twelve gates facing the four cardinal points: East, North, West, and South, according to the sacred text (21:13). The same iconographical scheme shows clearly the square form of the city: "And the city lieth foursquare, and the length is as large as the

The Heavenly Jerusalem, the Apocalypse of Saint-Séver, 11th century

His copies were taken to all parts of Spain that were not under the spiritual jurisdiction of Toledo, and beyond Spain to the rest of Europe. Until now, the very beautiful but very late Beatus manuscript from Saint-Séver in the Bibliothèque Nationale in Paris has been the one best known and most frequently studied. Another manuscript, now in the Pierpont Morgan Library in New York, is nearer to the original. More or less complete versions are to be found in Madrid, Valladolid, Seo de Urgel, Santo Domingo de Silos, Burgo de Osma, in the Escorial, in Lisbon,

breadth…" (21:16). The Heavenly Jerusalem is in fact the "squaring" of the heavenly cycle, its twelve gates corresponding to the twelve months of the year, as well as to the analogous divisions of the greater cycles, such as the precession of the equinoxes which, in the ancient world-system, is the greatest of all the astronomical cycles and therefore the largest measure of time. The Apocalypse mentions "twelve thousand furlongs" as the measure of the city's circuit; this number corresponds to the "great year" of the Persians and is in fact an approximate measure for half the equinoxial cycle, namely for the time of the reversion of the equinoxes (12960 years). Upon the walls of the heavenly city are seen twelve angels, who are the guardians of the gates (21:12), and under each gate is portrayed one of the twelve apostles, whose names are written on the city's foundations (21:14). Under the gates there are also represented twelve circles or spheres with inscriptions referring to the twelve precious stones garnishing the foundations of the wall (21:9). In older manuscripts of the same group, however, these circles clearly represent the pearls of which the gates are made: "And the twelve gates were pearls: every several gate was of one pearl" (21:21).

In the midst of the city the divine Lamb is standing; on his right we see the Evangelist, and on his left the Angel with the golden reed measuring the city (21:15).

For the medieval viewer it would have been clear that the city was in fact not only a square but a cube: "The length and the breadth and the height of it are equal" (21:16). The Heavenly Jerusalem is really a crystal, not only because of its transparent, incorruptible, and luminous substance, but also because of its crystalline form. It is the "crystallization," in the eternal present, of all the positive and essentially indestructible aspects of the temporal or changing world.

The Heavenly Jerusalem, the Morgan Beatus, 10th century, one of the most richly illustrated Spanish manuscripts associated with Beatus of Liébana's Commentary to the Apocalypse

Turin, Rome, Berlin, and in the British Museum. The two richest and best manuscripts of the whole group are the so-called Codex of Facundus in the National Library of Madrid and the Codex at the Cathedral of Gerona in Catalonia. The former was written for King Ferdinand I of Catalonia by his scribe Facundus and completed in 1047. It expresses, in its somewhat heraldic style, both the ceremonial and terrifying splendor suitable for the occasion. The Gerona manuscript, however, is older. It is dated 975, and represents the Mozarabic style of painting in its prime—as yet uninfluenced by Frankish art.

The Apocalypse of Gerona

We stood by the great table in the chapter house of the Cathedral of Gerona and opened the manuscript of the Apocalypse. In spite of the apocalyptic beasts, the dragons and scorpions, in spite of the severe angels, the burning cities and dying men and women, the first impression the pictures made on us was one of gay festivity, conjured up by their glowing color and purity of line. More than a hundred miniatures decorate the text. Most of them fill a whole page and some even spread to a whole opening, their backgrounds divided into great strips of color like a carpet on which the apocalyptic visions are developed: "And there appeared a great wonder in heaven; a woman clothed with the sun, and the moon under her feet, and upon her head a crown of twelve stars.…"

"And there appeared another wonder in heaven; and behold a great red dragon, having seven heads and ten horns, and seven crowns upon his heads. And his tail drew the third part of the stars of heaven, and did cast them to the earth.…" Across two pages a great red dragon glides diagonally, his tail stretching into the sky and one of his heads rearing in front of a woman dressed in the raiments of the sun, while from another head branching off below, a dark blue stream issues. There is no vision too great to be represented by the painters of this manuscript. They showed them in a literal and uninhibited way as usually only children can—and at the same time with a masterly control of line and mass. It does not matter that all the faces are identical, as if the same sign for "face" was valid in each and every case, because such a limitation only serves to emphasize the purely symbolic character of the paintings.

The archivist of the Cathedral, Don Jaime, explained the meaning of the miniatures to us, that open the whole work. On the verso of the first leaf, like a preface, is shown the

The Woman Clothed with the Sun, the Serpent, and the Child, the Beatus of 975, folios 171 and 172, Gerona

"Cross of Oviedo," which the north Spanish Christians carried with them as a Palladium in their first successful battle against the Muslims at Cavadonga in 718.

The Harvest of the Corn and the Grapes, the Beatus of 975, folios 193v and 194r, Gerona

Adoration of the Serpent and Beast, the Beatus of 975, folio 215v, Gerona

Opposite, on the right-hand side, one sees the Pantocrator, the ruler of the universe enthroned, holding the "mundus," the world, represented by a small sphere or disc, in two fingers of his right hand.

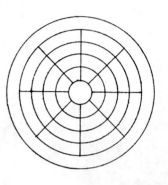

On the following opening, the hierarchy of the universe is shown in the form of concentric circles, in which the figures of genii, spirits, and angels are painted. Those in the outer circles belong to the terrestrial spheres, while those towards the middle belong to the celestial—for at the center, Christ himself appears in His divine form. From the outermost circle, emanating from eight human beings, eight rays or spokes reach towards the center. Christ's words written on these spokes identify them as the spiritual virtues, or the ways by which the spirit can overcome his worldly limitations and reach union with the Divine. Don Jaime is of the opinion that the representation of the universe in the form of concentric circles divided by eight "spokes" is derived from an Islamic model. Indeed, in the works of Islamic mysticism the same geometric scheme can be found described as the "Spider's Web of God." But on the other hand, this symbol is primeval and distributed throughout the whole world. How else could one depict more clearly that all being, in that it descends from the spiritual to the material, is farther and farther removed from the divine center and yet retains a link with that center always and everywhere? The pages following these are a history of mankind summarized in tables and pictures.

Then appears a page with a large peacock-like bird, who pierces a snake with his beak. The motif could have been derived from Islamic ceramics and one would be tempted to see only an ornament in it, were it not for the textual explanation that appears on the verso of the page. It speaks of a miraculous bird that lives in the Orient and hunts snakes. In order to deceive his prey, he covers his tail with clay and hides his radiant face behind it, as one would behind a shield. When the snake approaches, he strikes with his beak and splits its skull. In the same way, Christ hides his divine nature in human clay in order to defeat the ancient enemy, the serpent of the underworld. On the opposite side one sees a large A, made up of interlaced ribbons and covering almost the whole page. Two herons, that might almost be derived from Chinese silks, face each other under a roof made of the cross-piece of the A. Above this, Christ is enthroned with his hand raised as if he were to say "I am Alpha and Omega, the Beginning and the End." At this point, the archivist opened the last page of the book and showed the Omega, which also nearly fills the entire page. Under it the scribe entered the following words, read to us in ringing Latin by Don Jaime: "Senior presbiter scripsit,

Letter Alpha, the Beatus of 975, folio 216r, Gerona

Angels Carrying the Gospel,
the Beatus of 975, folio 6

Dominicus abbas liber fieri praecepit. Ende pintrix et dei aiutrix, frater Emeterius et presbiter": "The priest Senior wrote it. The abbot Dominicus had the book made. Ende, painter and handmaiden of God and Emeterius, brother and priest." So it was a woman who, together with Pater Emeterius, painted the miniatures. Whether she was a nun or a lady of the world, we do not know. He continued to translate: "The book was happily completed on Tuesday, the sixth of July. At this time, Fernando Flaginiz of Villas, the Toledan city, made war against the kingdom of the Moors. One counts the year 1003 of the Spanish era—that is, the year 975 according to today's reckoning...." The manuscript must have been made somewhere in Northern Spain, said Don Jaime, in an area in which one made war continuously against the Muslims. It could not have been produced in Catalonia because at that time the Visigothic script, in which the manuscript is written, was not in use. Catalonia was the bridgehead of Frankish influence south of the Pyrenees. In spite of that, the manuscript was in Gerona already in the Middle Ages, the archivist assured us, who seemed to be much concerned to emphasize the early ownership of the manuscript by the Cathedral of Gerona. He produced a document, the will of a canon and "Caput scholarum," who in the year 1078 bequeathed to the church of Gerona a precious commentary on the Apocalypse. That must have been our book, which this important canon perhaps obtained in León or Astorga and brought to Gerona, on the return from a pilgrimage to Santiago de Compostela. In any event, one knew the manuscript in Gerona in the twelfth century, when some of its miniatures were used as models for the sculptural decoration of the church and the cloisters. To show us examples of this influence by the manuscript, the canon led us into the wonderful inner cloister of the cathedral, whose columned walls surrounded a square "Paradise" planted with trees and bathed in sunlight. The capitals on columns supporting the arches are decorated with carvings, showing Biblical scenes and fantastic animals, which in their gentle but precise modelling betray the French influence of the School of Cluny. This was a world in which the pictures and the symbols of the Beatus manuscript were bound to find an echo. After the twelfth century, however, the manuscript seems to have been forgotten. No evidence exists of its presence in Gerona. Only in the year 1512, an entry in the "Green Book" of the Cathedral makes a short mention of the fact that the bishops ordered that the old manuscript of the Apocalypse be rebound. That is all. At that time, one began to despise medieval works of art. A new art, wholly intent on the exact rendering of the visual world, had begun to tread a victorious path, while an intoxicating hope, which was aroused by the discovery of the "New World," drew the mind away from the symbols which were enshrined in the pictures of the old manuscript. To the contemporaries of Columbus, the map of the world which one can see in our manuscript must have appeared childish and out of date, with its rectangular land mass around the Mediterranean surrounded by the ocean. Spain had become the world power on which, as Charles

The Burning Babylon, the Beatus of 975, folio 1215v, Gerona

V claimed, "the sun never set." Even when the reverse came to pass, as the proud Armada which was intended to restore the world dominion of the Catholic faith, was destroyed and every man in Spain was horrified by the unbelievable sentence pronounced by God, one did not pay any renewed attention to the old book and its symbols, perhaps because its pictures seemed barbaric.

Then came a period of strife, the unsuccessful attempts by the Catalans to free themselves from Spanish rule.

The Napoleonic armies occupied the country and the people rose in revolt. The time of the "guerillas," with all its horror mirrored by Goya, followed. Gerona was a center of the resistance against Napoleon. For three months it was besieged, three months of need, of hunger, and of heroic struggle by all its inhabitants. But then they had to submit. Napoleon's commissaries paid no attention to the old "barbaric" book.

Only around 1900, a Spanish scholar "discovered" the manuscript again, and now one began to value it more and more. After the first world war, European artists were also beginning to be attracted by it, finding in it a fully matured artistic expression which renders pictorial form in pure line and areas of primary colour. It was not the meaning of the pictures that were of interest to the painters but their apparently fantastic compositions. At that time, the German scholar Wilhelm Neuss, who was the first to examine the connection between all the Beatus manuscripts methodically, also came to Gerona. He thought the Gerona manuscript superior in beauty to all others.

Then came the civil war. The canons had to flee or to hide to avoid being killed. The cathedral was desecrated by the Reds. Even the relics of St. Narcissus, the founder saint of Gerona, were dragged from the sarcophagus, handed to the rabble, and burnt or thrown away. The manuscript of the Apocalypse remained untouched; it still lies there, unchanged over the centuries, recording and anticipating all past and future horrors in its pictures, which in spite of their terrifying details arouse neither fear nor revulsion because they are permeated by the serene melody of faith in Eternity.

Opposite: Jesus as the Lamb of God Standing on Mount Zion, the Fanlo Beatus, c. 1000
Right: The Triumphant Christian Warrior, the Beatus of 975, folio 134v, Gerona

The Foundations of Christian Art

I

The mysteries of Christianity were revealed in the heart of a world that was both chaotic and pagan. Its "light shone in the darkness" but was never able to transform completely the environment of its expansion. It is for this reason that Christian art, compared with that of the age-long civilizations of the East, is curiously discontinuous, both in its style and in its spiritual quality. Islamic art succeeded in realizing a certain degree of formal homogeneity only by rejecting out of hand the artistic heritage of the Graeco-Roman world, at least in the domains of painting and sculpture. The problem did not present itself in the same way to Christianity: Christian thought, with its emphasis on the person of the Savior, demanded a figurative art, so that Christianity was unable to set aside the artistic heritage of antiquity; but in adopting it, Christianity assimilated some germs of naturalism in the anti-spiritual sense of the word. Despite the long process of assimilation which that heritage underwent in the course of centuries, its latent naturalism never failed to break through every time there was a weakening of spiritual consciousness, even well before the Renaissance, when the definite break with tradition took place.[1] Whereas the art of the traditional civilizations of the East cannot properly be said to be split into sacred art and profane art, since sacred models inspire even its popular expressions, the Christian world has always known, side by side with an art that is sacred in the strict sense of the word, a religious art using more or less "worldly" forms.

The art that springs from a genuinely Christian inspiration is derived from certain images of the Christ and of the Virgin that have a miraculous origin. The craft traditions continue alongside it, and they become Christian by adoption; they are none the less sacred in character, in the sense that their creative methods embody a primordial wisdom that responds spontaneously to the spiritual truths of Christianity. These two currents, the traditional art of icon painting and the craft traditions, together with certain liturgical music evolved from a Pythagorean inheritance, are the only elements in Christian civilization that deserve to be called "sacred art."

The tradition of the sacred image, the "true icon" (*vera icon*) is essentially theological, and its origins are at once historical and miraculous, in conformity with the particular nature of Christianity; more will be said about this later. It is not at all surprising that the filiation of this art should be lost to our eyes in the obscurity

---

[1] The same can be said of the germs of philosophical rationalism latent in Christian thought; this is a striking corroboration of what has just been said about art.

Masons and Sculptors, French miniature, 15th century

of the pre-Constantinian period, since the origin of so many traditions that are recognized as apostolic is similarly lost in the same relative obscurity. Certain reservations were doubtless made during the earlier centuries of Christianity about figurative art, reservations conditioned both by the Judaic influence and by the contrast with the ancient paganism; for as long as the oral tradition was alive everywhere and Christianity had not yet come into the full light of day, the figuration of Christian truths in art can only have played a very occasional part, and then for special reasons. But later on, when social freedom on the one hand and the needs of the collectivity on the other encouraged religious art or even made it necessary, it would have been very strange if the tradition, with all its spiritual vitality, had not endowed this possibility of manifestation with all the spirituality that is compatible with its nature.

As for the craft tradition, with its pre-Christian roots, it is above all cosmological, for the work of the craftsman imitates quite naturally the formation of the cosmos out of chaos; its vision of the world is therefore not immediately connected with the Christian revelation, Christian language not being *a priori* cosmological. But the integration of the craft symbolism into Christianity was nevertheless a vital necessity, for the Church had need of plastic arts in order to clothe itself with visible forms, and it could not appropriate to itself the crafts without taking into account the spiritual possibilities they contain. Furthermore, the craft symbolism was a factor of equilibrium in the psychic and spiritual economy of the Christian "city"; it compensated so to speak the unilateral pressure of Christian morality, fundamentally ascetic as it is, by manifesting divine truths in a light that is relatively non-moral and in any case non-volitive: it sets up against the sermon which insists on what must be done by one who would become holy, a vision of the cosmos which is holy through its beauty;[2] it makes men participate naturally and almost involuntarily in the world of holiness. By the very fact that Christianity cleansed the craft inheritance of the factitious accretions imposed on it by Graeco-Roman naturalism, drunk as it was with human glories, it released the perennial elements retained in that inheritance, elements that re-enact the laws of the cosmos.[3]

The point of junction between the purely Christian tradition, which is theological in essence, and pre-Christian cosmology can be clearly discerned in the Christian signs in the Catacombs, and particularly in the monogram in the form of a wheel with six or eight spokes. It is well known that this monogram, the use of which dates from the earliest times, is made up of the Greek letters χ and ρ (Chi and Rho), either alone or combined with a cross. When this sign is inscribed in a circle it clearly assumes the form of the cosmic wheel; sometimes it is replaced by a plain cross inscribed in a circle. There can be no doubt about the solar nature of the last mentioned sign: in some Christian inscriptions in the Catacombs the circle emits rays having hands, an element derived from the solar emblems of ancient Egypt. Furthermore through the loop of the ρ which adorns the vertical axis like a polar star, the monogram combined with the cross shows a relationship to the looped cross, the Egyptian *ankh*.

The Christic monogram from the Catacombs, after Oskar Beyer

The wheel with eight spokes formed by the combination of the monogram and the cross, is analogous to the "rose of the winds," the diagram of the four cardinal directions and the four intermediate directions of the heavens.

[2] "Gnosis, by virtue of the very fact that it is a 'knowing' and not a 'willing,' is centered on 'that which is' and not on 'that which ought to be.' It gives rise to a view of the world and of life that differs widely from the view, more 'meritorious' perhaps but less 'true,' adopted by the volitive outlook with respect to the vicissitudes of existence" (Frithjof Schuon, *Gnosis: Divine Wisdom*, Bedfont, Perennial Books, 1959, chap. "Gnosis: Language of the Self").

[3] It is noteworthy that the general shape of the Christian temple does not perpetuate that of the Graeco-Roman temple, but the shapes of the basilica with apse and of domed buildings. The latter do not appear in Rome until a relatively late period. The interior of the Pantheon, with its immense dome taking in the light from above through a "solar eye," is not without grandeur, but this is neutralized by the anthropomorphic and commonplace character of the details. It has a sort of philosophical grandeur perhaps, but it is a grandeur that has nothing to do with contemplation.

A fact that must never be lost sight of is that to the ancients as well as to the people of the Middle Ages physical space, envisaged in its totality, is always the objectivation of "spiritual space." In truth it is nothing else, because its logical homogeneity resides as much in the spirit of the knower as in physical reality.

The monogram of the Christ is very often placed between the letters alpha and omega, symbolizing the beginning and the end. The combination of the cross, the monogram, and the circle signify the Christ as spiritual synthesis of the universe. He is the all, He is the beginning, the end, and the timeless center; He is the "victorious" and "invincible" sun (*sol invictus*); His Cross rules the cosmos,[4] it judges the cosmos. Because of this the monogram is also the sign of victory. The Emperor Constantine, whose position as supreme monarch in itself symbolized the *sol invictus*, inscribed this sign on his standard, thereby announcing that the cosmic purpose of the Roman Empire was fulfilled in the Christ.

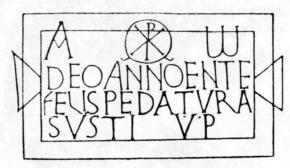

Paleo-Christian inscription from the Catacombs, with the Christic monogram between the Alpha and Omega. The solar circle of the monogram has "hands of light," following an Egyptian design. After Oskar Beyer

The Christ is also likened to the *sol invictus* in the liturgy, and the orientation of the altar confirms this assimilation. The liturgy, like many of the ancient mysteries, recapitulates the drama of the divine sacrifice in conformity with the general significance of the regions of space and the cyclical measures of time. The cosmic image of the Word is the sun.

The integration into Christianity of the craft traditions, with all their cosmological outlook, had been providentially prepared for by the institution of the solar calendar by Julius Caesar,[5] who had drawn inspiration from Egyptian science; also by the transposition of the Julian calendar and of the principal solar feasts into the Christian liturgical year. It must never be forgotten that reference to the cosmic cycles is fundamental in the craft traditions and especially in architecture; this operation indeed gives the impression of a real "crystallization" of the celestial cycles. The significance of the directions of space cannot be dissociated from that of the

Christ as *Sol Invictus*, detail from the Mausoleum of the Julii, Rome, late 3rd century

---

[4] In the Orthodox feast of the Elevation of the Cross, the liturgy exalts the universal power of the Cross, which "makes to flower anew the incorruptible life, and confers deification on creatures, and brings the devil finally to the ground." In these words the analogy of the tree of the world, changeless axis of the cosmos, can be discerned.

[5] It will be remembered that Dante made Caesar the artisan of the world destined to receive the light of the Christ.

phases of the solar cycle; this is a principle common to ancient architecture and to the liturgy.

Christian architecture perpetuates the fundamental diagram of the cross inscribed in the circle. It is significant that this design is at the same time the symbol of the Christ and the synthesis of the cosmos. The circle represents the totality of space, and therefore also the totality of existence, and at the same time the celestial cycle, the natural divisions of which are indicated by the cross of the cardinal axes and are projected into the rectangular shape of the temple. The plan of a church emphasizes the form of the cross, and it corresponds not only to the specifically

Apse mosaic from St. Apollinare in Classe, Ravenna, c. 549

Christian meaning of the cross, but also to its cosmological role in pre-Christian architecture. The cross of the cardinal axes is the mediating element between the circle of the sky and the square of the earth: and it is the Christian perspective in particular that gives first place to the part played by the Divine Mediator.

II

The symbolism of the Christian temple rests on the analogy between the temple and the body of the Christ, in accordance with the following words from the Gospel: "Jesus answered and said unto them, 'Destroy this temple and in three days I will raise it up.' Then said the Jews, 'Forty and six years was this temple in building, and wilt thou rear it up in three days?' But he spake of the temple of his body" (John 2:19-21).

The temple of Solomon, replaced before the Christian era by the temple of Zorobabel, was the dwelling-place of the *Shekhina*, the Divine Presence on earth. According to the Jewish tradition, this Presence withdrew from the earth after the fall of Adam, but returned to inhabit the bodies of the patriarchs. Later on Moses prepared for it a movable dwelling in the tabernacle, and, in a more general sense, in the body of the purified people of Israel.[6] Solomon built for it a fixed habitation, in accordance with the plan revealed to his father David: "Thus spake Solomon, 'The Lord said that he would dwell in the thick darkness. I have surely built thee an house to dwell in, a settled place for thee to abide in for ever'" (I Kings 8:12-13). "And now, O God of Israel, let thy word, I pray thee, be verified, which thou spakest unto thy servant David my father. But will God indeed dwell on the earth? Behold the heaven and heaven of heavens cannot contain thee; how much less this house that I have builded" (I Kings 8:26-27). "Now when Solomon had made an end of praying, the fire came down from heaven, and consumed the burnt offering and the sacrifices; and the glory of the Lord filled the house. And the priests could not enter into the house of the Lord, because the glory of the Lord had filled the Lord's house" (II Chron. 7:1-2).

The temple of Solomon was to be replaced by the body of the Christ:[7] when He died on the Cross the curtain before the holy of holies in the temple was rent. The body of the Christ is also the Church in its aspect as the communion of saints: the symbol of this Church is the Christian temple.

The Fathers of the Church say that the sacred building represents first and foremost the Christ as Divinity manifested on earth; at the same time it represents the universe built up of substances visible and invisible, and finally, man and his various "parts."[8] According to some of the Fathers the holy of holies is an image of

[6] The nomadic life, the absence of a fixed sanctuary, and the prohibition of images are related to the purification of the people of Israel.

[7] According to St. Augustine, Solomon built the temple as "type" of the Church and of the body of the Christ (*Enarr. in Ps.* 126). According to Theodoret, the temple of Solomon is the prototype of all the churches built in the world.

[8] St. Augustine compares the temple of Solomon with the Church, the stones of which it is built being the believers, and its foundations the prophets and the apostles; all these elements are joined

Crucifix from the Church of Santa Chiara, Assisi, 12th century

Cathedral of Monreale, 12th century

the Spirit, the nave is an image of reason, and the symbol of the altar summarizes both;[9] according to others the holy of holies, that is to say the choir or the apse, represents the soul, while the nave is analogous to the body, and the altar to the heart.[10]

Some medieval liturgists, such as Durant de Mende and Honorius d'Autun, compare the plan of the cathedral to the form of the Crucified: His head corresponds to the apse with its axis to the East, His outstretched arms are the transepts, His torso and legs are at rest in the nave, His heart lies at the principal altar. This interpretation recalls the Hindu symbolism of *Purusha* incorporated in the plan of the temple; in both cases the Man-God incarnated in the sacred building is the holocaust who reconciles Heaven with earth. It is conceivable that the Christian interpretation of the plan of the temple is an adaptation to the Christian perspective of a symbolism much more ancient than Christianity; but it is equally possible, and perhaps more probable, that two analogous spiritual conceptions were born independently one of the other.

together by Charity (*Enarr. in Ps.* 39). This symbolism was developed by Origen. St. Maxim the Confessor sees in the church built on earth the body of the Christ, as well as man and the universe.
[9] Maxim the Confessor adopts this point of view.
[10] This is St. Augustine's point of view. See also Simeon of Thessalonica, *De divino Templo*, Patrologia Migne.

Church of Santa Constanza, Rome, 4th century

It will be observed that the Hindu symbolism expresses the divine manifestation in a generalized way. The *Vastu-Purusha-mandala* is a diagram of the relation Spirit-matter or essence-substance, whereas the Christian parable of the temple envisages in particular the "descent" of the Word in human form. The metaphysical principle is the same but the sacred messages differ.

The Royal Portal of Chartres Cathedral

The Royal Portal of the Cathedral of Chartres, with its three bays opening towards the West, reveals three different aspects of the Christ, and these are also aspects of the temple itself, identified as it is with the body of the Christ. The left-hand bay, situated to the North of the central bay is dedicated to the Christ ascending to Heaven; the right-hand bay, situated to the South of the central bay, is dedicated to the Virgin and to the nativity of the Christ; the central bay, the real "Royal gate," presents the Christ in Glory, according to the apocalyptic vision of St. John. Thus the two niches on the left and on the right, corresponding respectively to the northern

Central bay of the Royal Door

and southern sides of the church, represent, in conformity with the symbolism of the solstitial "gates"—the gate of winter and the gate of summer—the celestial nature and the terrestrial nature of the Christ. As for the central bay, it symbolizes for all time the one and only door, which transcends cyclical antitheses and reveals the Christ in His Divine Glory, appearing as judge of all things at the final reintegration of this "age" in the timeless.

The figure of the Christ in Glory surrounded by the tetramorph fills the central tympanum. The composition is limpid and radiant, and its balance, held between the almond-shaped aureole of the Christ and the slightly ogival arch of the tympanum, seems alive, as if it were breathing calmly, swelling from the center and returning to it. The four and twenty elders of the Apocalypse occupy the covings, sitting on thrones and wearing crowns and separated from the tympanum by a rank of angels; on the lintel the twelve apostles are portrayed.

The tympanum of the right-hand bay is dominated by the statue of the Virgin and Child, sitting on a throne and directly fac-

The Royal Portal of Chartres Cathedral, 12th century

ing the spectator, between two archangels swinging censers, in accordance with a Byzantine tradition. Their movement, like that of doves on the point of flight, accentuates by contrast the majestic immobility of the Virgin between them. The composition of this lunette is the reverse of that of the ascension of the Christ, in which the angels are leaning outwards, like petals dropping from a flower. Below this group—at once severe and joyful—of the Virgin and archangels are the following scenes, in two horizontal bands: the Annunciation, the Visitation, the Nativity, and the Presentation in the Temple. The lowest point of the tympanum, which is not separated from the lintel, is occupied by the Virgin lying on her bed; the bed has a flat roof over it, and on this roof is the cradle with the Child. This unusual peculiarity can be explained by the parallelism of the three superposed groups. At the lowest point the Virgin lying horizontally, beneath the newborn infant, symbolizes perfect humility, and therefore also the pure passivity of Universal Substance, the *materia prima* which is entirely receptive with respect to the Divine Word. In the band immediately above, and on the same vertical axis, the Infant Jesus standing upright on the altar of the temple accentuates the analogy between the Virgin and the altar of sacrifice; higher up, in the arch of the tympanum, the Virgin seated on the throne and holding the Infant in her lap corresponds to the Universal Mother, who is the humble foundation of all creatures and at the same time their most sublime substance, as is indicated by Dante in his well known prayer addressed to the Virgin: *Vergine madre, figlia del tuo figlio, umile ed alta più che creatura* [Virgin Mother, daughter of thy Son, lowly and exalted more than any creature]... (*Paradiso*, XXXIII, 1 sqq.).

The Door of the Virgin, right-hand tympanum of the Royal Door

According to the teaching of the Fathers the incarnation of the Word as such is a sacrifice, not only by virtue of the Passion, but more especially because the Divinity is brought to an extreme of "humiliation" by the descent into a human and terrestrial form. It is true that God as God, in His eternal Essence, does not undergo the sacrifice; however, since the suffering of the Divine Man would not carry its real significance were it not for the presence of the Divine Nature in Him, the burden of the sacrifice does nevertheless in a certain sense fall in the end on God, whose infinite love embraces both the "height" and the "depth." Similarly in the Hindu doctrine, *Purusha* as Supreme Being cannot be subject to the limitations of the world in which and through which He manifests Himself; none the less, He can be regarded as taking on those limitations, because they are contained as possibilities in His own infinity.

These considerations are not taking us away from our subject. They are helpful towards an understanding of how close is the linkage that joins the meaning of the temple as body of the Divine Man with its cosmological meaning, for the cosmos represents in its most general significance the "body" of the revealed Divinity. It is at this point that the initiatic doctrine of the ancient "freemasons" meets Christology.

It is known that the proportions of a church were usually derived from the harmonious division of a great circle, that is to say, its division into five or into ten. This Pythagorean method, which the Christian builders had probably inherited from the *collegia fabrorum*,[11] was employed not only in the horizontal plane but also in a vertical plane,[12] so that the body of the building was as it were inscribed in an imaginary sphere. The symbolism thus produced is very rich and very adequate to the requirements of the situation: the crystal of the sacred building is coagulated out of the indefinite sphere of the cosmos. This sphere is also like an image of the universal nature of the Word, whose concrete and terrestrial form is the temple.

Division into ten parts does not fit in with the purely geometrical nature of the circle, for the compass divides it into six and into twelve; it corresponds however to the cycle, of which it indicates the successively decreasing phases, according to the formula $4 + 3 + 2 + 1 = 10$. This method of establishing the proportions of a building therefore partakes of the nature of time, so that it is not misleading to say that the proportions of a medieval cathedral reflect a cosmic rhythm. Moreover, proportion is in space what rhythm is in time, and in this connection it is significant that harmonious proportion is derived from the circle, the most direct image of the celestial cycle. In this way the natural continuity of the circle is to a certain extent introduced into the architectural order, the unity of which becomes to that extent non-rational, and not comprehensible within the limits of the purely quantitative order.

[11] See Paul Naudon, *Les Origines religieuses et corporatives de la Franc-Maçonnerie*, Paris, Dervy, 1953.
[12] See E. Moessel, *Die Proportion in Antike und Mittelalter*, München, C. H. Beck'sche Verlagsbuchhandlung, 1926.

Opposite: Christ in Majesty, fresco at the Abbey of Berzé-la Ville, early 12th century

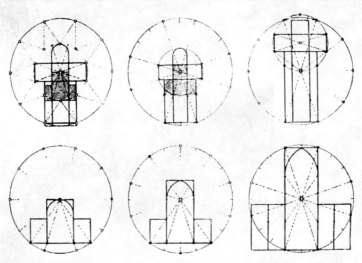

Examples of the proportions of medieval churches, after Ernst Moessel

The fact that a sacred edifice is an image of the cosmos implies *a fortiori* that it is an image of Being and its possibilities, which are as it were "externalized" or "objectivized" in the cosmic edifice. The geometrical plan of the building therefore symbolizes the "Divine Plan." At the same time it represents the doctrine, which each artisan collaborating in the work of construction could conceive and interpret within the limits of his particular art; it was a doctrine at once secret and open.

Like the cosmos the temple is produced out of chaos. The building materials, wood, brick, or stone, correspond to the *hyle* or *materia prima*, the plastic substance of the world. The mason dressing a stone sees in it the *materia* which will participate in the perfection of the world only to the extent that it takes on a *forma* determined by the Spirit.

The tools used to shape the crude materials accordingly symbolize the divine "instruments" which "fashion" the cosmos out of the undifferentiated and amorphous *materia prima*. In this connection it is worth recalling the fact that in the most diverse mythologies, tools are identified with divine attributes; this explains why the initiatic transmission in the craft initiations was closely linked with the care of the tools of the craft. It can therefore be said that the tool is greater than the artist, in the sense that its symbolism goes beyond the individual as such; it is like an outward sign of the spiritual faculty linking the man to his divine prototype, the *Logos*. Moreover tools are analogous to weapons, which are also often treated as divine attributes.[13]

Thus the tools of the sculptor, the mallet and chisel, are in the likeness of the "cosmic agencies" which differentiate primordial matter, represented in this case by the unworked stone. The complementarism of the chisel and the stone necessarily reappears elsewhere and in other forms in most traditional crafts, if not in all. The plough works the soil[14] as the chisel works the stone, and in a similar way and

[13] First among divine instruments—and weapons—is lightning, which symbolizes the Word or the Primordial Intellect, and is in its turn symbolized by ritual scepters, such as the *Vajra* in Hindu and Buddhist iconography. The legendary power of certain famous swords is also significant in this connection.

Master Mason Supervising Stone Cutting

in a principial sense, the pen "transforms" the paper;[15] the instrument that cuts or shapes always appears as the agent of a male principle which acts on a female material. The chisel corresponds very evidently to a faculty of distinction or discrimination; active with respect to the stone, it becomes passive in its turn when it is considered in connection with the mallet, to the "impulsion" of which it is subject. In its initiatic and "operative" application the chisel symbolizes a distinctive knowledge and the mallet a spiritual will that "actualizes" or "stimulates" that knowledge. Here the cognitive faculty is situated below the volitive faculty, and this seems at first sight to contradict the normal hierarchy, but the apparent reversal is explained by the fact that the principial relation, in which knowledge has precedence over will, necessarily undergoes a metaphysical inversion in the "practical" domain. It is moreover the right hand that wields the mallet and the left that guides the chisel.

Plowman at Work, Flemish miniature, 14th century

[14] The art of ploughing is often considered as having a divine origin. Physically the act of ploughing the ground has the effect of opening it to the air, thus promoting the fermentation that is indispensable for the assimilation of the soil by vegetation. Symbolically the soil is opened up to the influences of Heaven, and the plough is the active agent or generative organ. It may be noted in passing that the replacement of the plough by machines has reduced many fertile soils to sterility and thus changed them into deserts; it is a case of the curse inherent in machines spoken of by René Guénon in his book *The Reign of Quantity and the Signs of the Times*, translated by Lord Northbourne, London, Luzac, 1954.

[15] The symbolism of the reed pen (*calamus*) and the book, or the pen and the tablet, plays a very important part in the Islamic tradition. According to the doctrine of the Sufis the "supreme *calamus*" is the "Universal Intellect," and the "guarded tablet" on which the *calamus* writes the destiny of the world corresponds to the *Materia prima*, the uncreated—or non-manifested—"Substance," which under the influence of the "Intellect" or the "Essence" produces everything comprised in the "creation." See the author's book, *An Introduction to Sufi Doctrine*, Lahore, Ashraf, 1959.

The Scribe Eadwine, from the Canterbury Psalter, c. 1150

Sculptor, bronze doors of San Zeno Maggiore Church, Verona

Goldsmiths, Flemish, 14th century

A Painter, English, c. 1350

Weavers, Flemish, 14th century

Pure principial knowledge, which could be called "doctrinal"—and the "discernment" in question is no more than its practical or "methodical" application—does not intervene "actively," or shall we say "directly," in the work of spiritual realization but orders it in conformity with changeless truths. This transcendent knowledge is symbolized in the spiritual method of the stone-carver by the various measuring instruments, such as the plumb line, the level, the square, and the compass, images of the changeless archetypes which preside over all the phases of the work.[16]

By analogy with certain craft initiations that still exist today in the East, it may be supposed that the rhythmical activity of the stone-carver was sometimes combined with the invocation, voiced or silent, of a divine name. In such a case the name, considered as a symbol of the creating and transforming Word, would be like a gift bequeathed to the craft by the Jewish or Christian tradition.

What has just been said about the work of the carver makes it clear that the initiatic teaching transmitted in the craft corporations must have been "visual" rather than "verbal" or "theoretical." The practical application of elementary geometrical principles alone must have awakened spontaneously some "presentiments" of metaphysical realities in artisans with a gift for contemplation. The use of measuring instruments, regarded as spiritual "keys," would then help towards an understanding of the ineluctable rigor of the universal laws, first in the "natural" order, through the observation of the laws of statics, and then in the "supernatural" order, by an intuition, through the said laws, of their uni-

[16] It could equally well be said that these instruments correspond to the different "dimensions" of knowledge. See Frithjof Schuon, *The Transcendent Unity of Religions*, London, Faber & Faber, 1953, chap. "Conceptual Dimensions."

Musician, German, 13th century

Parchment Maker, German, 13th century

versal archetypes: presupposing always that the "logical" laws, which are derived from the rules of geometry and of statics, had not up to that time been arbitrarily enclosed within the limits of the notion of matter to such an extent that confusion with the inertia of the "non-spiritual" could arise.

Conceived in this way, the work of the artisan becomes a rite; nevertheless, if it is really to have the quality of a rite it must have some attachment to a source of Grace. The link that unites the symbolical act with its divine prototype must become the channel of a spiritual influence, so that it may bring about an intimate "transmutation" of the consciousness; it is indeed known that the craft initiation comprised a quasi-sacramental act of spiritual affiliation.

The goal of a realization attained by way of art or artisanship was "mastery," that is to say a perfect and spontaneous command of the art, a mastery in practice coinciding with a state of interior liberty and veracity. This is the state that Dante symbolizes as the earthly paradise situated on the summit of the mountain of purgatory. When he arrived at the threshold of this paradise, Virgil said to Dante, "Henceforth expect no more my words nor my counsel, for your judgment is free, upright, and sound, and it would be a fault not to obey it; I declare thee also master of thyself, with the crown and the miter."[17] Virgil personifies the pre-Christian

---

[17] *Non aspettar mio dir più, nè mio cenno; Libero, dritto, e sano è tuo arbitrio, E fallo fora non fare a suo senno, Per ch'io te sopra te corono e mitrio* (*Purgatorio*, XXVII, 138-140).

Dante and Beatrice Approaching the Sun, illumination by Giovanni di Paolo, 15th century

wisdom that guides Dante through the psychic worlds to the center of the human state, the Edenic state from which begins the ascent to the "heavens," symbols of supra-formal states. The ascent of the mountain of purgatory corresponds to the realization of what were called in antiquity the "Lesser Mysteries," while the climb to the celestial spheres corresponds to a knowledge of the "Greater Mysteries." The symbolism used by Dante is mentioned simply because it gives a very clear idea of the range of a cosmological initiation such as a craft initiation.[18]

It is important not to lose sight of the fact that in the eyes of every artist or artisan taking part in the building of a church, the theory was visibly being made manifest by the building as a whole, reflecting as it did the cosmos or the Divine plan. Mastery therefore consisted in a conscious participation in the plan of the "Great Architect of the Universe." It is this plan that is revealed in the synthesis of all the proportions of the temple; it coordinates the aspirations of all who take part in the work of the cosmos.

It could be said in quite a general way that the intellectual element in the method was manifested in the regular shape that had to be conferred on stone. For *forma* in the Aristotelian sense plays the part of "essence"; it is *forma* that recapitulates in a certain sense the essential qualities of a being or of an object, and is thus opposed to *materia*. In the initiatic application of this idea, the geometrical models represent aspects of spiritual truth, while the stone is the soul of the artist. The work done on the stone, consisting in the removal of all that is superfluous and in conferring a "quality" on something that is still no more than a crude "quantity," corresponds to the development of the virtues, which in the human soul are the supports and at the same time the fruits of spiritual knowledge. According to Durandus de Mende, the stone "trimmed to a rectangle and polished" represents the soul of a

[18] See René Guénon, *L'Esotérisme de Dante*, Paris, Les Editions Traditionnelles, 1939.

holy and steadfast man who will be built into the wall of the spiritual temple by the hand of the Divine Architect.[19] According to another parable, the soul is changed from a crude stone, irregular and opaque, into a precious stone, penetrated by the Divine Light which it reflects through its facets.

Demiurge (God as Architect), miniature from the *Bible moralisée*, c. 1250

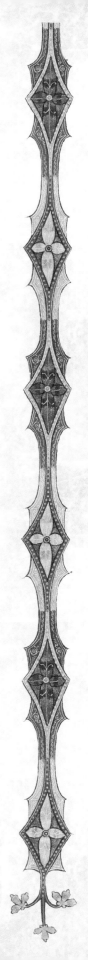

[19] According to the words of the Apostle: "Ye also, as lively stones, are built up a spiritual house" (I Peter 2:5).

Two Examples of Christian Symbolism

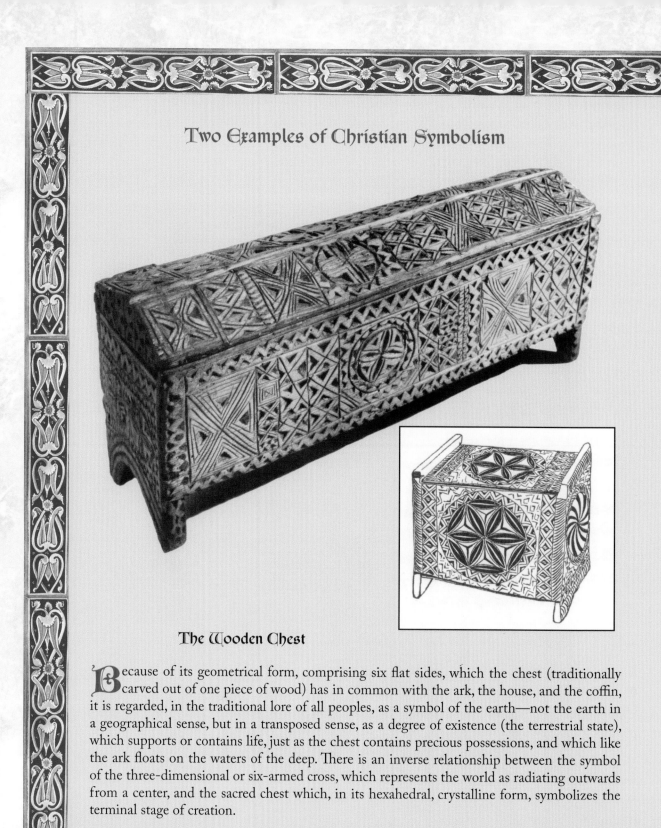

The Wooden Chest

Because of its geometrical form, comprising six flat sides, which the chest (traditionally carved out of one piece of wood) has in common with the ark, the house, and the coffin, it is regarded, in the traditional lore of all peoples, as a symbol of the earth—not the earth in a geographical sense, but in a transposed sense, as a degree of existence (the terrestrial state), which supports or contains life, just as the chest contains precious possessions, and which like the ark floats on the waters of the deep. There is an inverse relationship between the symbol of the three-dimensional or six-armed cross, which represents the world as radiating outwards from a center, and the sacred chest which, in its hexahedral, crystalline form, symbolizes the terminal stage of creation.

Gargoyles

The purpose of the grotesque masks on the outside walls of Romanesque churches was undoubtedly that they should serve as a means of exorcism against impure spirits. The mode of action of such exorcistic masks can be readily understood if one considers how, when a man approaches a sanctuary and seeks to direct his spirit towards the highest, all the dregs in his being, owing to a natural reaction of the soul, tend to arise and seek to enter his thoughts under a multitude of guises. If, at this moment, he espies a mask which represents, with unmistakable grossness, any hidden greed, passivity, or lust, he can look on them "objectively," and laugh at them. In this way the evil spirit is exorcized and flees the scene.

These stone masks thus contribute to a process of unmasking in the soul, but on a basis that is the exact opposite of modern psychoanalysis. For whereas in the latter the one who is plagued by dubious impulses is invited to accept his complexes as himself, the medieval man, awakened by an exorcistic device, looks on the mischievous intruder as an enemy from without, as an impulse foreign to himself which, like a disease, has sought to take root in him, and which he has only to perceive with clarity in order to be freed from it. For, according to Christian doctrine, the devil cannot tolerate the truth.

Above: Gargoyles in the Cathedral of St. Rumbald, Mechelen, Belgium
Right: Gargoyle in Lichfield Cathedral, England

III

Forma and *materia* were familiar terms in medieval thought; they have been intentionally chosen here to designate the poles of a work of art. Aristotle, who referred the nature of every being or object to these two basic principles, used the artistic procedure for the purposes of his demonstrations, for the two principles in question are not *a priori* logical determinations, they are something more. Thought does not deduce them but presupposes them; their conception is not essentially founded on rational analysis, but on intellectual intuition, the normal support of which is not argument but the symbol; the clearest symbol of this ontological complementarism is precisely the relation between the model or the idea (*eidos*) which pre-exists in the mind of the artist, and the material, be it wood, clay, stone, or metal, that is to receive the imprint of that idea. Without the example of plastic material, ontological *materia* or *hyle* cannot be conceived, for it is not measurable nor definable; it is "amorphous," not only in the relative sense in which the material of a craft is "amorphous" or crude, but also in a radical sense, for it is without intelligibility of any kind until it is joined to a *forma.* Correspondingly, although *forma* may be up to a point conceivable as such, it is nevertheless not imaginable apart from its union with *materia*, which determines it by lending it an "extension" either subtle or quantitative. In short, although the two ontological principles, once they have been recognized, are intellectually evident, it is no less true that the concrete symbolism provided by the work of the artist or craftsman cannot be dispensed with for their demonstration. Moreover, since the range of the symbolism extends far beyond the domain of reason, one must conclude that Aristotle borrowed the notions of *eidos* and *hyle*, translated by the Latins into *forma* and *materia*, from a real tradition, that is to say, from a method of teaching derived at once from doctrine and from Divine art.

It is also worthy of note that the Greek word *hyle* literally means wood; wood is in fact the principal material used in the crafts of archaic civilizations. In certain Asiatic traditions, notably in Hindu and Tibetan symbolism, wood is also regarded as a "tangible" equivalent of the *materia prima,* the universal plastic substance.

The example of art, taken by Aristotle as a conceptual starting point, is only fully valid if the reference is to traditional art, wherein the model, which by analogy plays the part of "formal" principle, is truly the expression of an essence, that is to say of a synthesis of transcendent qualities. In the practice of any such art this qualitative essence is embodied in a symbolical formulation susceptible of many "material" applications. According to the material receiving the imprint of the model, the model will reveal either more or less of its intrinsic qualities, just as the essential form of a being is either more or less in evidence according to the plastic capacity of its *materia.* On the other hand, it is form that brings out the particular nature of a material, and in this connection also traditional art is more truthful than a naturalistic or illusionist art, which tends to dissimulate the natural characteristics of plastic materials. Let us recall once more that the relation *forma-materia* is such that *forma* becomes measurable only through its combination with *materia*, whereas *materia* is intelligible only by virtue of *forma.*

Individual existence is always woven of *forma* and *materia*, simply because the polarity they represent has its foundation in Being itself. Indeed *materia* proceeds from *materia prima*, the universal passive substance, while *forma* corresponds to the active pole of Being, the essence: when essence is referred to in connection with a particular being, it represents the archetype of that being, its permanent possibility in the Spirit or in God. It is true that Aristotle does not make this last transposition; he does not relate *forma* back to its metacosmic principle, no doubt because he consciously limits himself to the domain accessible to his method of demonstration; this domain is characterized by the possibility of a coincidence within it of ontological and logical laws. Nevertheless Aristotle's axioms, for example hylemorphic complementarism, presuppose a metacosmic background, such as medieval thought discerned quite naturally in the Platonic point of view. The doctrines of Plato and of Aristotle contradict one another on the rational plane alone; if one understands the myths of Plato, they cover the aspect of reality to which Aristotle confines his attention. Those who represent the highest development of the Middle Ages were therefore right in subordinating the perspective of Aristotle to that of Plato.[20]

The Medieval Universe, after a French manuscript of the 14th century

[20] Albert the Great wrote: "Know that one does not become an accomplished philosopher save by knowing the two philosophies of Aristotle and of Plato" (Cf. E. Gilson, *La Philosophie au moyen âge*,

Boethius Discussing Music with Pythagoras, Plato, and Nichomachus,
12th century

Whether one accepts the doctrine of Plato in its characteristic dialectical form, or whether one feels obliged to reject it, it is impossible from the Christian point of view to deny that the essential possibilities of all things are eternally contained in the Divine Word, the Logos. For "all things were made" by the Word (John 1:3), and in It alone—or through It—are all things known, since It is the "true Light, that lighteth every man that cometh into the world" (John 1:9-10). Therefore the light of the intellect does not belong to us, it belongs to the omnipresent Word; and this light contains essentially the qualities of knowable things, for the innermost reality of the cognitive act is quality, and quality is "form," understood in the Peripatetic sense of the word. "The form of a thing," says Boethius, "is like a light by which that thing is known."[21] This is the eminently spiritual significance of hylemorphism: the "forms" of things, their qualitative essences, are in themselves transcendent; they can be found at all levels of existence; it is their coincidence with this or that material—or with some modality of the *materia prima*—which delimits them and reduces them to their more or less ephemeral "traces."

Boethius has just been quoted; in the Middle Ages he was one of the great masters of art, and it was he who handed on the Pythagorean idea of art.[22] His treatise on the *quadrivium* is more than a mere exposition of the minor arts—arithmetic, geometry, music, and astronomy—it presents a real science of form, and it would be a mistake not to recognize the extent of its applicability to the plastic arts. In Boethius' eyes all the formal orders are "demonstrations" of the ontological Unity. His arithmetic represents not so much a method of calculation as a science of number, and he does not see number *a priori* as a quantity, but as a qualitative determination of unity, like the Pythagorean numbers themselves, which are analogous to the Platonic "ideas": duality, the ternary, the quaternary, the quinary, etc., represent so many aspects of Unity. That which links

Paris, Payot, 1944, p. 512). Similarly, St. Bonaventura said: "Among the philosophers, Plato received the word of Wisdom, Aristotle that of Science. The former considered principally superior reasons, the latter inferior reasons" (Cf. St. Bonaventura, works presented by Father Valentin—M. Breton, Aubier, Paris, 1943, p. 66). The Sufis were of the same opinion.

[21] Cf. Anicius Manlius T. S. Boethius, *De Unitate et Uno*, Patrologie Migne.

[22] Together with Isidore of Seville and Martianus Cappella.

the numbers together is essentially proportion, which in its turn is a qualitative expression of Unity; the quantitative aspect of numbers is merely their material "development."

The qualitative unity of number is more evident in geometry than in arithmetic, for quantitative criteria are not really sufficient to distinguish between two figures such as the triangle and the square, each of which has its unique and so to speak inimitable quality.

Proportion is in space what harmony is in the realm of sound. The analogy subsisting between these two orders is demonstrated by the use of the monocord, the string of which produces sounds that vary according to the length of its vibrating part.

Arithmetic, geometry, and music correspond to the three existential conditions of number, space, and time. Astronomy, which is essentially a science of cosmic rhythms, comprehends all these domains.

It may be noted that the astronomy of Boethius has been lost. His geometry as we know it has many gaps; perhaps we should only see in it a sort of summary of a science which must have undergone a considerable development in the workshops of the medieval builders, not to mention the cosmological speculations which accompanied it.

Whereas modern empirical science considers first of all the quantitative aspect of things, while detaching it as far as possible from all its qualitative connotations, traditional science contemplates qualities independently of their quantitative associations. The world is like a fabric made up of a warp and a weft. The threads of the weft, normally horizontal, symbolize *materia* or, more immediately, such causal relations as are rationally controllable and quantitatively definable; the vertical threads of the warp correspond to *formae*, that is to say to the qualitative essences of things.[23] The science and the art of the modern period are developed in the horizontal plane of the "material" weft; the science and the art of the Middle Ages on the other hand are related to the vertical plane of the transcendent warp.

[23] See also René Guénon, *The Symbolism of the Cross*, London, Luzac, 1958, chap. "The Symbolism of Weaving."

Personification of the *Quadrivium*, from the *Arithmetic* of Boethius, c. 845

IV

The sacred art of Christianity constitutes the normal setting of the liturgy, of which it is an amplification in the fields of sound and of sight. Like the non-sacramental liturgy, its purpose is to prepare and to bring out the effects of the means of grace instituted by the Christ Himself. When Grace is in question no environment can be "neutral"; it will always be for or against the spiritual influence; whatever does not "assemble" must inevitably "disperse."

It is quite useless to invoke "evangelical poverty" in order to justify the absence or the rejection of a sacred art. True enough, when the Mass was still celebrated in caverns or catacombs, sacred art was superfluous, at least in the form of plastic art; but from the time when sanctuaries began to be built they had to be subject to the rules of an art conscious of spiritual laws. Not a single primitive or medieval church in fact exists, poor though it be, the forms of which do not bear witness to a consciousness of that kind,[24] whereas every non-traditional environment is encumbered with forms that are empty and false. Simplicity is in itself one of the marks of tradition, whenever it is not just the simplicity of virgin nature.

The liturgy itself can be thought of as a work of art comprising several degrees of inspiration. Its center, the Eucharistic sacrifice, belongs to the order of Divine Art; through it is accomplished the most perfect and the most mysterious of transformations. Spreading outwards from this center or kernel, like an inspired but necessarily fragmentary commentary, is the liturgy, founded on usages consecrated by the Apostles and the Fathers of the Church. In this connection, the great variety of liturgical usages, such as existed in the Latin Church before the Council of Trent, in no way hid the organic unity of the work, but on the other hand emphasized its internal unicity, the divinely spontaneous nature of the plan and its character as art in the highest sense of the word; it is for this very reason that art properly so called was all the more easily integrated with the liturgy.

It is by virtue of certain objective and universal laws that the architectural environment perpetuates the radiancy of the Eucharistic sacrifice. Sentiment, however noble its impulse, can never create such an environment, for affectivity is subject to the reactions engendered by reactions, it is wholly dynamic, and cannot apprehend directly or with any certainty the qualities of space and time which correspond quite naturally to the eternal laws of the Spirit. It is impossible to be engaged in architecture without becoming implicitly engaged in cosmology.

The liturgy does not determine the architectural order alone, it also regulates the disposition of sacred images according to

[24] Certain churches built within ancient Greek or Roman sanctuaries may be regarded as exceptions; but they are "exceptions" in a very relative sense, since sanctuaries alone are in question.

Ethiopian processional cross, 16th century

First Lindau book cover, St. Gall, late 8th century

Iconostasis, Cathedral of the
Annunciation, Moscow, 1489
Opposite: Nave of the Cathedral
of St. Mark, Venice, 1094

the general symbolism of the regions of space and the liturgical significance of left and right.

It is in the Eastern Orthodox Church that images are most directly integrated with the liturgical drama. They adorn more particularly the iconostasis, the barrier that divides the Holy of Holies—the place of the Eucharistic sacrifice enacted under the eyes of the priests alone—from the nave to which the majority of the faithful have access. According to the Greek Fathers the iconostasis is the symbol of the limit that separates the world of the senses from the spiritual world, and that is why the sacred images appear on that barrier, just as the Divine Truths which reason cannot directly apprehend are reflected in the form of symbols in the imaginative faculty, which is intermediate between the intellect and the sensorial faculties.

The plan of Byzantine Churches is distinguished by a division into a choir (*adyton*) to which the priests, with their attendant deacons and acolytes, alone are admitted, and a nave (*naos*) which shelters the rest of the community. The choir is relatively small; it does not form a single unit with the nave which holds without respect to persons the whole crowd of believers standing with the iconostasis in their full view. The iconostasis has three doors, by which the officiants go in and out as they announce the various phases of the divine drama. The deacons use the lateral doors; only the priest at special moments such as the carrying of the consecrated elements or the book of the Gospels may pass through the Royal Door, the central one, which is thus made an image of the

Right: The original Byzantine plan of the Cathedral of St. Mark, Venice, after Ferdinand Forlati

Nave of Sainte-Madeleine, Vézelay, 12th century

solar or Divine door.[25] The *naos* is usually more or less concentric in shape, a shape that corresponds to the contemplative character of the Eastern Church: space is as it were gathered in on itself, while still expressing the limitlessness of the circle or the sphere.

The Latin liturgy on the other hand tends to differentiate architectural space according to the cross formed by the axes, and thus to communicate to it something of the nature of movement. In Romanesque architecture the nave gets progressively longer; it is the way of pilgrimage to the altar, to the Holy Land, to Paradise; the transept too is developed more and more extensively. Later on Gothic architecture emphasizes to the utmost extent the vertical axis, and ends by absorbing the horizontal development into one great leap towards Heaven. The various branches of the cross are gradually incorporated into a vast nave, with perforated partitions and diaphanous outer walls.

The crypt and the cave are the models of Latin sanctuaries at the height of the Middle Ages; these sanctuaries are concentrated on the Holy of Holies, the vaulted apse, enclosing the altar as the heart holds the Divine Mystery; their light is the light of the candles on the altar, as the soul is illumined from within.

Gothic cathedrals realize a different aspect of the mystical body of the Church, or of the body of man sanctified, namely his transfiguration by the light of Grace. So diaphanous a condition in architecture only became possible with the differentiation of structural elements into ribs and membranes, the ribs assuming the static function and the membranes that of clothing. Here there is in a certain sense a passage from the static condition of the mineral world to that of the vegetable world; it is not for nothing that Gothic vaulting recalls the calyces of flowers. There is also the fact that a "diaphanous" architecture would not be possible without the art of the glazier, whose windows make the outer walls transparent while safeguarding the intimacy of the sanctuary. The light broken up by stained glass is no longer that of the crudity of the outer world, it is the light of hope and beatitude. At the same time the color of the glass has itself become light, or more exactly, the light of day reveals its inward richness through the transparent and sparkling color of the glass; so the

Crypt of Notre-Dame du Fort d'Étampes, Essonne, France, 12th century

[25] It has been asserted that the traditional form of the iconostasis, with its little columns framing the icons, was derived from the stage of the ancient theatre, which had a back wall similarly adorned with pictures and pierced by doors through which the actors entered and left. If there is any truth in this analogy, it is because the form of the ancient theatre was related to a cosmic model, so that the doors at the back of the stage are like the "gates of Heaven," by which the gods descend to earth and souls ascend to Heaven.

Sainte-Chapelle, Paris, 1243-1248

Divine Light, which as such is blinding, is attenuated and becomes Grace when it is refracted in the soul. The art of staining glass conforms closely to the Christian genius, for color corresponds to love, as form corresponds to knowledge. The differentiation of the one and only light by the many-colored substances of the windows recalls the ontology of the Divine Light as expounded by a St. Bonaventure or a Dante.

The dominant color of the window is blue, the blue of the depth and the peace of the sky. Red, yellow, and green are used sparingly, and thereby seem all the more precious; they suggest stars or flowers or jewels, or drops of the blood of Jesus. The predominance of blue in medieval windows produces a light that is serene and soft.

In the pictography of the great cathedral windows the events of the Old and New Testaments are reduced to their simplest formulation, and are enclosed within a geometrical framework. They thus appear as prototypes eternally contained within the Divine Light; light is crystallized. Nothing is more joyous than this art; how remote it is from the somber and tormented imagery of some Baroque churches!

Considered as a craft the art of staining glass is one of a group of techniques having as

their aim the transformation of materials, namely, metallurgy, enamelling, and the preparation of paints and dyes, including liquid gold. These techniques are all interconnected through a common craft inheritance which goes back in part as far as ancient Egypt, with alchemy as its spiritual complement; the crude material is the image of the soul which must be transformed by the Spirit. The transmutation of lead into gold in alchemy seems to involve a break of natural laws, but this is because it expresses in the language of the artisan the transformation, at once natural and supernatural, of the soul. The transmutation is natural because the soul is predisposed towards it, and supernatural because the real nature of the soul, or its true equilibrium, is in the Spirit, just as the real nature of lead is gold. But the passage from one to the other, from lead to gold, or from the unstable

Above: Detail from the James the Greater stained-glass window, Chartres Cathedral, 13th century
Right: Notre-Dame de la Belle Verrièrre, Chartres Cathedral, 12th century

and disunited ego to its incorruptible and single essence, is only possible by some sort of miracle.

The noblest manual craft put to the service of the Church is that of the goldsmith, for his is the craft that fashions the sacred vessels and ritual instruments. There is something solar in this art, gold being related to the sun; and therefore the utensils created by the goldsmith manifest the solar aspect of the liturgy. The various hieratic forms of the cross, for example, represent so many modalities of the divine radiance; the divine center reveals itself in the dark space that is the world.[26]

All arts founded on a craft tradition work to a geometrical or chromatic plan, which cannot be separated from the material processes of the craft, but retain none the less their character as symbolical "keys" that can open up the cosmic dimension of each phase of the work.[27] An art of this kind is therefore necessarily "abstract" through the very fact that it is "concrete" in its processes; the designs at its disposal will depend for their proper application both on expert craftsmanship and on intuition, but they will be transposable at need into a figurative language, which will retain something of the "archaic" style of the creations of craftsmanship. This is what happens in the art of staining glass, and the same is the case with Romanesque sculpture, which is derived directly from the art of the mason; it keeps the technique and the rules of composition of that art, while reproducing at the same time models derived from the icon.

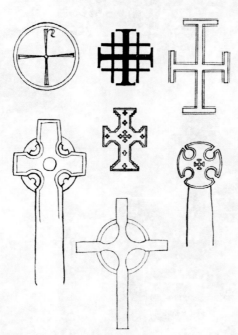

Different hieratic forms of the Cross

[26] These various forms of the cross all saw the light during the earliest centuries of Christianity. Sometimes the radiating aspect of the cross predominates, and sometimes the static or square aspect, these two elements being combined in different ways with the circle or the disc. The cross of Jerusalem for instance, with branches ending in lesser crosses, suggests the omnipresence of Grace by the multiple reflection of the divine center, while at the same time it mysteriously links the cross with the square. In Celtic Christian art the cross and the solar wheel are united in a synthesis full of spiritual evocations. The hieratic shapes of the tiara and the miter also recall solar symbols. As for the staff of the bishop, it ends either in two opposed serpents' heads like the caduceus, or in a spiral; the latter is sometimes stylized in the form of a dragon with its jaws open towards the paschal lamb; it is then an image of the cosmic cycle "devouring" the sacrificial victim, the sun or the Man-God.

[27] For example, the cross inscribed in a circle, which can be regarded as the key figure in sacred architecture, represents also the diagram of the four elements grouped round the "quintessence," and linked together by the circular movement of the four natural qualities: heat, humidity, cold, and dryness, which correspond to the subtle principles governing the transmutation of the soul in the alchemical sense. Thus the physical, psychic, and spiritual orders are brought into correspondence in a single symbol.

Opposite: The "Cross of Victory," Oviedo Cathedral, Spain, 908

The Portal of St. Gall, Basle Cathedral

The Portal of St. Gall

The portal of the North transept of the cathedral of Basle, commonly called the "portal of St. Gall" (*Galluspforte*, corresponding to the patronymic of the adjacent chapel), is a work in the purest Romanesque style. It has all the static equilibrium of that style and all its serene structural unity, although it is situated, historically speaking, on the threshold of the Gothic era.

The tympanum is dominated by the figure of the Christ seated between St. Peter and St. Paul, who intercede with Him on behalf of their protégés, the donor and the builder of the portal. The Christ carries the standard of the Resurrection in His right hand and the open book in His left hand. To this figure of the Christ as victor and judge are related, as to an ideal center, the group of the four Evangelists, whose effigies, surmounted by the four beasts of the Apocalypse, are carved between the pillars of the door in such a way as to be incorporated in the outer angles of the stepped splay. This arrangement, which recalls the painted decoration of certain apses, is made more complex by the addition of a second figure of the Christ to the lintel of the doorway, where He is represented as the divine bridegroom who opens the door to the wise virgins while turning his back on the foolish ones.

The portal properly so called is framed in a sort of external porch, consisting of small pavilions placed one above the other. This has been compared to the architectural facing of a Roman triumphal arch. In two of the pavilions that are bigger than the others are statues of St. John the Baptist and St. John the Evangelist; the traditional association of these two saints is related to the presence of the Christ in the tympanum in the same way as the alpha and omega of the ideograms are related to the Christic symbol. Above these two statues, in two other pavilions of the external porch, are two angels sounding the trumpet of the Resurrection; at the side of each, men and women leave their graves and put on their clothing; beneath the two St. Johns, and up to the height of the uprights of the portal, six other pavilions or tabernacles contain reliefs representing works of charity. To these, the principal elements of the figured ornamentation, are added other ornaments in the shape of animals and plants.

The niche of the portal corresponds to the choir of the church. Like the choir it is the place of the divine epiphany, and as such it conforms to the symbolism of the celestial door, which is not only the entry through which souls pass into the Kingdom of Heaven, but also the way out by which the divine messengers "descend" into the "cave" of the world. This symbolism is of pre-Christian origin, and becomes as it were integrated with Christianity through the celebration of Christmas—the night of the birth of the Divine Sun into the world—approximately at the winter solstice, the "Gate of Heaven."

The portal with niche is thus an iconostasis which simultaneously both hides and reveals the mystery of the Holy of Holies, and in this connection it is also a triumphal arch and a throne of glory.

V

The tradition of the sacred image is related to established prototypes which have a historical aspect. It comprises a doctrine, that is to say, a dogmatic definition of the sacred image, and an artistic method which allows the prototype to be reproduced in a manner conformable to its meaning. The artistic method in its turn presupposes a spiritual discipline.

Among the prototypes generally handed down in Christian art, the most important is the *acheiropoietos* ("not made by human hands") image of the Christ on the *Mandilion*. It is said that the Christ gave His image, miraculously imprinted on a piece of fabric, to the messengers of the King of Edessa, Abgar, who had asked Him for His portrait. The *Mandilion* had been preserved at Constantinople until it disappeared when the town was pillaged by the Latin Crusaders.[28]

Another prototype, no less important, is the image of the Virgin attributed to St. Luke; it is preserved in numerous Byzantine replicas.

Latin Christianity too possesses models consecrated by tradition, such as for example the Holy Countenance (*Volto Santo*) of Lucca, which is a crucifix carved in wood, Syrian in style, attributed by legend to Nicodemus the disciple of Christ.

Attributions such as these naturally cannot be proved historically; perhaps they ought not to be taken literally, but should be interpreted as having the function of confirming the authority of the traditional sources in question. As for the usual traditional representation of the Christ, its authenticity is confirmed by a thousand years of Christian art, and this alone is a powerful argument in favor of

The *Mandilion*, Russian icon

[28] A copy of the *Mandilion* is preserved in the cathedral of Laon.

that authenticity, for, unless reality is denied to everything of that order, it must be admitted that the Spirit present in the tradition as a whole would soon have eliminated a false physical representation of the Savior. The representations of the Christ on certain sarcophagi of the period of Roman decadence evidently prove nothing to the contrary, any more than do the naturalistic portraits of the Renaissance, for the latter are no longer within the Christian tradition, while the former had not yet entered it. It may also be noted that the imprint preserved on the Holy Shroud of Turin, the details of which have only been made clearly visible by modern methods of investigation, resembles in a striking way, so far as characteristic details are concerned, the *acheiropoietos* image.[29]

The above remarks on the traditional icon of the Savior are equally applicable to the icon of the Virgin attributed to St. Luke. Some other types of icon—such as that of the "Virgin of the Sign" which represents the Holy Virgin in an attitude of prayer with a medallion of the

The *Volto Santo*, Lucca

Christ Emmanuel on her breast, or such as the figure compositions which once adorned the walls of the Church of the Nativity in Bethlehem—are convincing, in the absence of any tradition establishing their origin, by reason of their spiritual quality and their evident symbolism, which testify to their "celestial" origin.[30] Certain variations of these prototypes have been "canonized" in the Eastern Orthodox Church, on account of miracles worked through their intervention, or because of their doctrinal or spiritual perfection;[31] these variations have in their turn become prototypes for icons.

[29] If this imprint were the work of a painter, it would be impossible to attribute it either to an ancient or medieval artist, or to an artist of modern times. Against any such attribution are, in the first case, the absence of stylization, and in the second, the depth of the spiritual quality, not to mention historical reasons. It is anyhow out of the question that an image of such spiritual veracity should be the outcome of a fraud.

[30] The most ancient example of the "Virgin of the Sign" dates from the fourth century; it was found in the Roman catacomb of the Cimitero Maggiore. The same composition became very famous in the form of the *Blacherniotissa*, a miraculous Virgin of Constantinople.

[31] This last case is that of the celebrated picture by St. Andrei Rublev representing the three Angels visiting Abraham. The motive as such goes back to palaeo-Christian art; it constitutes the only traditional iconograph of the Holy Trinity. (Cf. L. Ouspensky and V. Lossky, *The Meaning of Icons*, Boston, The Boston Book and Art Shop, 1956.)

It is very significant for Christian art, and for the Christian point of view in general, that these sacred images have a miraculous origin, and thus one that is mysterious and at the same time historical. This fact moreover makes the relation between the icon and its prototype very complex: on the one hand the miraculous image of the Christ or of the Virgin is to the work of art what the original is to the copy; on the other hand the miraculous portrait is itself no more than a reflection or a symbol of an eternal archetype, in this case the real nature of the Christ or of His mother. The situation of art is here strictly parallel to that of faith; for Chris-

tian faith is connected in practice to a clearly defined historical event, the descent of the Divine Word to earth in the form of Jesus, though it has also essentially a non-historical dimension. Is not the decisive quality of faith its acceptance of the eternal Realities of which the event in question is one of the expressions? To the extent that spiritual consciousness grows less and the emphasis of faith is directed to the historical character of the miraculous occurrence rather than to its spiritual quality, the religious mentality turns away from the eternal "archetypes" and attaches itself to historical contingencies, which thereafter are conceived in a "naturalistic" manner, that is to say, in the manner that is most accessible to a collective sentimentality.

An art that is dominated by spiritual consciousness tends to simplify the features of the sacred image and to reduce them to their essential characteristics, but this in no way implies, as is sometimes suggested, a rigidity of artistic expression. The interior vision, oriented towards the celestial archetype, can always communicate to the work its subtle quality, composed of serenity and plenitude. On the other hand in periods of spiritual decadence the naturalistic element inevitably shows through. This element was in any case latent in the Greek inheritance of Western painting, and its incursions, threatening the unity of the Christian style, made themselves felt well before the "Renaissance." The danger of "naturalism" or an arbitrary exaggeration of style, replacing the spiritual imponderables of the pro-

totype by purely subjective features, became all the more real because collective passions, held in check by the unalterable character of the scriptural traditions, found an outlet in art. This is as much as to say that Christian art is an extremely fragile thing, and that it can only retain its integrity at the cost of ceaseless watchfulness. When it becomes corrupted, the idols which it then creates react in their turn, on

Above: The Great *Panaghia*, Yaroslavl, 12th century
Opposite: *Madonna and Child on a Curved Throne*, Greece, 13th century

The Holy Trinity, St. Andrei
Rublev, c. 1411

the whole in a predominantly harmful way, on the collective mentality. When this has happened neither the opponents nor the partisans of the religious image need ever be short of valid arguments, because the image is good in one aspect and bad in another. However that may be, a sacred art can never be safeguarded without formal rules and without a doctrinal consciousness in those who control and inspire it; consequently the responsibility falls on the priesthood, whether the artist be a simple artisan or a man of genius.

The Byzantine world only became conscious of all that is implied in sacred art as a consequence of the disputes between iconoclasts and iconodules, and to a large extent thanks to the threatening approach of Islam. The uncompromising attitude of Islam towards images necessitated something like a metaphysical justification of the sacred image on the part of the Christian community in danger, all the more so because the Islamic attitude appeared to many Christians to be justified by the Decalogue. This became the occasion for recalling that the veneration of the image of the Christ is not only permissible, but that it is also the manifest testimony of the most essentially Christian dogma: that of the incarnation of the Word. God in His transcendent Essence cannot be represented, but the human nature of Jesus which He received through His mother is not inaccessible to representation; moreover the human form of the Christ is mysteriously united with His Divine Essence, despite the distinction of the two "natures," and this justifies the veneration of His image.

At first sight this apologia for the icon appears to be concerned only with its existence and not with its form; nevertheless the argument just quoted implies the development of a doctrine of the symbol, which must determine the whole orientation of art: the Word is not merely the pronouncement, at once eternal and temporal, of God, it is equally His image, as St. Paul said;[32] that is to say, It reflects

[32] Cf. Col. 1:15: "*Qui est imago Dei invisibilis, primogenitus omnis creaturae* [Who is the image of the invisible God, the firstborn of every creature]...."

God on every level of manifestation. The sacred image of the Christ is thus only the final projection of the descent of the Divine Word to earth.[33]

The VIIth council of Nicea (AD. 787) established the justification of the icon in the form of a prayer addressed to the Virgin who, as the substance or the support of the incarnation of the Word, is also the true cause of its figuration: "The indefinable (*aperigraptos*) Word of the Father made Himself definable (*periegraphe*), having taken flesh of Thee, O Mother of God, and having refashioned the image (of God) soiled (by original Sin) to its former estate, has suffused It with Divine beauty. But confessing salvation we show it forth in deed and word."

The principle of symbolism had already been demonstrated by Dionysius the Areopagite:[34] "The sacerdotal tradition, as well as the divine oracles, hides that which is intelligible beneath that which is material, and that which surpasses all beings beneath the veil of these same beings; it gives form and likeness to that which has neither form nor likeness, and through the variety and materiality of these emblems it makes multiple and composite that which is excellently single and incorporeal" (*Of Divine Names*, I. 4). The symbol, he explains, is two-faced: on one side it is deficient with respect to its transcendent archetype, to the point of being separated from it by all the abyss that separates the terrestrial world from the divine world; on the other side, it participates in the nature of its model, for the inferior proceeds from the superior; in God alone subsist the eternal types of all beings, and all are penetrated by the Divine Being and the Divine Light. "We see then that one can attribute likenesses to celestial beings without impropriety, though they be produced from the most lowly parts of matter, since this matter itself, having received its subsistence from absolute Beauty, preserves through all its material structure some vestiges of intellectual beauty, and since it is possible through the medium of this matter to raise oneself to the immaterial archetypes, provided that one is care-

The Ustyug Annunciation, Moscow, second half of the 12th century

[33] Cf. L. Ouspensky and V. Lossky, *The Meaning of Icons*.

[34] No purpose is served by depreciating, however indirectly, this great spiritual writer by inflicting on him the new surname of "Pseudo-Dionysius," whatever may be the value of recent historical theories.

The Transfiguration, School of Theophanes the Greek, Moscow, c. 1403

ful, as has been said, to look at the metaphors more particularly in the light of their unlikeness, that is to say, instead of considering them always in the same light, to take account of the distance that separates the intelligible from the sensible, and to define them in the way that most appropriately suits each of their modes" (*Of the Celestial Hierarchy*, I. 4).[35] But the dual aspect of the symbol is assuredly nothing else but the dual nature of form, understood, in the sense of *forma*, as the qualitative imprint of a being or a thing; for form is always a limit and at the same time the expression of an essence, and that essence is a ray of the Eternal Word, supreme archetype of all form and so of every symbol, as is shown by these words of St. Hierotheos, the great teacher quoted by Dionysius in his book on Divine Names: "As form giving form to all that is formless, in so far as It is the principle of form, the Divine Nature of the Christ is none the less formless in all that has form, since It transcends all form...." Here is the ontology of the Word in its universal aspect; the particularized and as it were personal aspect of the same Divine Law is the Incarnation, by which "the indefinable Word of the Father made Itself definable." This is expressed by St. Hierotheos in the following words: "Having condescended through love of man to assume man's nature, having really incarnated Itself...(the Word) nevertheless kept in this state Its marvelous and superessential nature. In the very midst of our nature It remained marvelous, and in our essence superessential, containing in Itself eminently all that belongs to us and comes from us, above and beyond ourselves."[36]

According to this spiritual view, the participation of the human form of the Christ in His Divine Essence is as it were the "type" of all symbolism: the Incarnation presupposes the ontological link which unites every form with its eternal archetype; at the same time it safeguards that link. Nothing remained but to relate this doctrine to the nature of the sacred image, and this was done by the great apologists of the icon, notably St. John Damascene,[37] who inspired the VIIth Council of Nicea, and Theodore of Studion, who finally clinched the victory over the iconoclasts.

In the *Libri Carolini* Charlemagne reacted against the iconodule formulae of the VIIth Council of Nicea, doubtless because he saw the danger of a new idolatry among Western peoples, who are less contemplative than Eastern Christians: he wanted the function of art to be didactic rather than sacramental. From this time onwards the mystical aspect of the icon became more or less esoteric in the West, while it remained canonical in the East, where it was also supported by monasticism. The transmission of sacred models continued in the West until the Renaissance, and even today the most celebrated miraculous images venerated in the Catholic Church are icons in the Byzantine style. The Roman Church could put forward no doctrine of the image in opposition to the dissolving influence of

---

[35] From the French translation by Maurice de Gandillac: *Oeuvres complètes du Pseudo-Denys l'Aréopagite*, Paris, Aubier, 1949.

[36] *Oeuvres complètes du Pseudo-Denys l'Aréopagite.*

[37] It is significant that St. John Damascene (700-750) lived in a small Christian community entirely surrounded by the Islamic civilization.

the Renaissance, whereas in the Eastern Orthodox Church the tradition of the icon has been carried on, though less intensively, right up to modern times.[38]

VI

The doctrinal foundation of the icon determines not only its general orientation, its subject and its iconography, but also its formal language, its style. This style is the direct result of the function of the symbol: the picture must not seek to replace the object depicted, which surpasses it eminently; according to the words of Dionysius the Areopagite it must "respect the distance that separates the intelligible from the sensible." For the same reason it must be truthful on its own plane, that is to say it must not create optical illusions, such as arise from a perspective in depth or a modeling that suggests a body projecting a shadow. In an icon the only perspective is the logical; sometimes the optical perspective is deliberately reversed; modeling by superimposed "lights," inherited from Hellenism, is reduced until it no longer disturbs the flat surface of the picture; often it is translucid, as if the persons represented were penetrated by a mysterious light.[39] There is no determinate illumination in the composition of an icon; instead the gold background is called "light," for it corresponds to the celestial Light of a world transfigured.[40] The folds of clothing, the arrangement of which is also derived from Greek antiquity, become the expression, not of physical movement, but of a spiritual rhythm: it is not the wind that swells the fabrics, it is the spirit that animates them. The lines no longer serve only to mark the contours of bodies, they acquire a direct significance, a graphic quality both limpid and supra-rational.

Much of the spiritual language of the icon is transmitted with the technique of icon painting which is organized in such a way that inspiration accompanies it almost spontaneously, provided that the rules are observed and that the artist himself is spiritually prepared for his task. This must be taken to mean, in a general sense, that the painter must be sufficiently integrated with the life of the Church; in particular, he must prepare himself for his work by prayer and fasting; he must meditate on the subject to be portrayed with the help of the canonical texts. When the subject chosen is simple and central, such as the image of the Christ alone or of the Virgin and Child, his meditation will be founded on one of the formulae or prayers that are of the essence of the tradition; in such a case the

The Virgin and the Child, Basilica of St. Clare, Assisi, 12th century

---

[38] The tradition nearly died out in the eighteenth century, but it seems to be coming to life again in a few widely separated places in our own days.

[39] This is related to the doctrine of the transfiguration of bodies by the light of Tabor, according to Hesychast mysticism. Cf. L. Ouspensky and V. Lossky, *The Meaning of Icons*.

[40] Cf. L. Ouspensky and V. Lossky, *The Meaning of Icons*.

Simone Martini

Simone Martini, *Virgin and Child*, 1320

Simone Martini, *The Annunciation*, 1333

Simone Martini, perhaps the greatest of all the Sienese painters, adopted a pronouncedly chivalrous and aristocratic style. In a mural painted by him in the great room in the Town Hall which he began in 1315, he shows the Holy Virgin with the Child sitting on Her throne under a wide tent-shaped canopy. She accepts the homage other attendant saints like a noble lady presiding at a "cour d'amour" [court of love]. In his work Simone Martini indicates space only in so far as it does not interfere with the harmony of outline and color. He lends to outline a restrained melodious flow and to color the translucence of spring. The great picture of *The Annunciation* in the Uffizi Gallery in Florence is also by his hand and in later years Martini was summoned to Avignon to decorate the Pope's palace.

Icon of the Holy Face "Not Made by Hands" (*acheiropoietos*), School of Novgorod, Russia, 12th century

traditional model of the icon, with its synthetic symbolism, will respond to the intellectual essence of the prayer and will reveal its virtualities. Indeed the schematic arrangement of the icon always affirms the metaphysical and universal background of the religious subject, and this incidentally proves the non-human origin of the models. Thus, for example, in most icons of the Virgin and Child the outlines of the Mother as it were envelop those of the Child; the mantle of the Virgin is often dark blue, like the measureless depth of the sky or like deep water, while the clothing of the Divine Child is royal red. All these details have a profound significance.

Along with the *acheiropoietos* image of the Christ, that of the Virgin and Child is the icon *par excellence*. The representation of the Child, whose nature is mysteriously divine, is in a sense justified by that of His Mother, who clothed Him with Her flesh. A polarity then becomes apparent between the two figures, full of natu-

The Holy Virgin of the Sign, Greek icon

ral attractiveness, but of inexhaustible significance: the nature of the Child is considered in relation to the nature of His Mother and as it were through Her nature; conversely, the presence of the Divine Child, with His attributes of royalty and wisdom—or of His future Passion—confers an impersonal and profound aspect on maternity: the Virgin is the model of the soul in its state of primordial purity, and the Child is like the germ of the Divine Light in the heart.

This mystical relationship between the Mother and the Child finds its most direct expression in the "Virgin of the Sign," the oldest examples of which date from the fourth or fifth century; the Virgin is depicted in the attitude of prayer with

Above: *The Nativity of Christ*, Novgorod, Russia, c. 1475
Right: St. Basil the Great, Macedonia, 1699

Her hands uplifted and with the medallion of the young Christ Emmanuel on Her breast. It is the "Virgin who shall be with child" according to the Prophet Isaiah, and it also the prayerful Church or soul in which God will manifest Himself.

The icons of saints find their doctrinal foundation in the fact that they are indirectly icons of the Christ: the Christ is present in man sanctified and "lives" in him, as the Apostle expresses it.

The principal scenes of the Gospels have been handed down in the form of type compositions; some of their features are related to the apocryphal Gospel of the Infancy. That the infant Jesus should be born in a cave, that the cave should be in a mountain, and that the star which announced His birth should send forth its ray like a vertical axis on to the cradle in the cave, all this implies nothing that does not correspond to a spiritual truth; and the same applies to the angels, the royal Magi, the shepherds and their flocks. A representation of this kind is in accordance with the sacred Scriptures, but it is not derived directly from them, and it could not be accounted for in the absence of a tradition to safeguard the symbolism.

It is significant that according to the Christian perspective eternal realities appear in the form of historical events, and this alone makes them accessible to representation. Thus, for example, the descent of the Christ into hell, conceived as an event occurring simultaneously with the death on the Cross, is really situated outside time: if the early patriarchs and prophets of the Old Testament cannot escape from the darkness except through the intervention of the Christ, it is because the Christ in question is really the Eternal Christ, the Word; the prophets had encountered it before its incarnation in Jesus. Nevertheless, since the death on the Cross is like the intersection of time and eternity in the life of Jesus, it is legitimate from a symbolical point of view to represent the risen Savior as descending, in His human form, into the antechamber of hell, where He smashes the gates and holds out His hand to the ancestors of humanity, the patriarchs and prophets assembled to welcome Him. Thus the metaphysical meaning of a sacred image is not contradicted by its childish or "ingenuous" appearance.

The Descent into Hell, Workshop of Dionysius, Moscow, 1495-1504

The Theological Message of Russian Icons

The art of icons is a sacred art in the true sense of the term: it is nourished wholly on the spiritual truth to which it gives pictorial expression. For this reason it is often inadequately and faultily judged when approached from the outside and with criteria borrowed from profane and purely human art.

Most studies on art place historical development in the forefront; they analyze the interplay of ethnic and geographical influences and seek thereby to explain the art itself, while the intellectual content of the pictorial representation plays a subordinate role. In the art of icons, however, it is the content that is the criterion of the form. The specifically doctrinal character of this art determines not only the iconography, but also its artistic form and general style. This is so because the meaning of an icon touches a center so close to man's essence that it governs virtually all aspects of the work of art, from its didactic elements to the imponderables of artistic inspiration.

It is quite different in profane art, where the subject matter of a painting merely provides an opportunity for the artist to express his own genius, which may be more vital than the subject chosen and whose richness comes from elsewhere.

It is through its content that a sacred art has access to a living and truly inexhaustible source. Hence it is in its nature to remain true to itself, even when a particular artist has not himself fully realized the spiritual depth of a given theme, and so does not draw directly from the spring of holiness, but only transmits more or less of the light that is comprised in the sacred forms sanctioned by Tradition.

Fundamentally, the icon always remains the same; changes of style arise from the meeting between the timeless spirit of tradition and circumstances conditioned by time and place, which merely cause the unfolding of diverse potentialities latent in the nature of the icon itself. As Leonid Ouspensky has rightly said,[41] just as Byzantium brought theology to a certain perfection in words, so Russia has done likewise in pictures.

Nothing could be more presumptuous than the wish to replace traditional wisdom with the point of view of modern psychology, which is quite out of place here. There is just as little possibility of grasping spiritual content psychologically as of explaining the nature of beauty psychologically.

[41] Cf. L. Ouspensky and V. Lossky, *The Meaning of Icons*.

Left: The Deesis, Pskov School, Russia, 13th century; *Right*: St. Tsarevitch Dimitri of Ouglitch, Russia, 17th century

The Decadence and the Renewal
of Christian Art

I

Awork of art, if it is to be of spiritual import, need not be a "work of genius"; the authenticity of sacred art is guaranteed by its prototypes. A certain monotony is in any case inseparable from traditional methods: amid all the gaiety and pageantry that are the privilege of art, this monotony safeguards spiritual poverty—the non-attachment of the "poor in spirit" (Matt. 5:3)—and prevents individual genius from foundering in some sort of hybrid monomania; genius is as it were absorbed by the collective style, with its norm derived from the universal. It is by the qualitative interpretation, to whatever degree, of the sacred models that the genius of the artist shows itself in a particular art; that is to say: instead of squandering itself in "breadth," it is refined and developed in "depth." One need only think of an art such as that of ancient Egypt to see clearly how severity of style can itself lead to extreme perfection.

This allows us to understand how, at the time of the Renaissance, artistic geniuses suddenly sprang up almost everywhere, and with an overflowing vitality. The phenomenon is analogous to what happens in the soul of one who abandons a spiritual discipline. Psychic tendencies that have been kept in the background suddenly come to the fore, accompanied by a glittering riot of new sensations with the compulsive attraction of as yet unexhausted possibilities; but they lose their fascination as soon as the initial pressure on the soul is relaxed. Nevertheless, the emancipation of the "ego" being thenceforth the dominant motive, individualistic expansivity will continue to assert itself; it will conquer new planes, relatively lower than the first, the difference in psychic "levels" acting as the source of potential energy. That is the whole secret of the Promethean urge of the Renaissance.

We must add, however, that the psychic phenomenon just referred to is not in every respect parallel to a collective phenomenon such as the Renaissance, since the individual implicated in a collective "fall" of that kind is not directly responsible for it, hence his relative innocence. Genius in particular often partakes of the quasi "natural" or "cosmic" innocence of the psychic forces that are unlocked by the great crises of history; this indeed is the source of its charm. Nonetheless, its influence is not any the less pernicious, to one degree or another.

Opposite: Cathedral of Strasbourg, West facade, 13th century
Right: Three figures from the central portal of the West front, Chartres Cathedral, 13th century

For the same reason, in every work of real genius—in the current and individualistic sense of the word—there are real values previously unperceived or neglected. It is necessarily so, since every traditional art obeys a particular spiritual economy that limits its themes and means of expression, so that an abandonment of that economy almost immediately releases new and apparently unlimited artistic possibilities. Nonetheless, such new possibilities can never henceforth be co-ordinated with respect to a single center; they will never again reflect the amplitude of the soul at rest within itself, in its "state of grace"; their tendency being centrifugal, their various modalities of vision and expression will be mutually exclusive and will succeed one another with ever-growing rapidity. Such in fact are the "stylistic periods," the dizzying succession of which is so characteristic of the European art of the last five centuries. Traditional art does not have this dynamism, but it is not for that reason "frozen": protected by the "magic circle" of sacred form, the traditional artist creates both like a child and like a sage: the models he reproduces are symbolically timeless.

In art as in everything else, man finds himself faced by the following alternative: he must seek the Infinite in a relatively simple form, keeping within the limits of that form and working through its qualitative aspect, while sacrificing some possible developments, or he must seek the Infinite in the apparent richness of diversity and change, though it must lead in the end to dispersion and exhaustion.

The economy of a traditional art can be more or less ample, it can be flexible or rigid; all depends on the power of spiritual assimilation inherent in a particular civilization, environment, or collective vocation. Racial homogeneity and historical continuity also have a part to play: millennial civilizations like those of India and China have been able, spiritually speaking, to integrate very diverse artistic possibilities—and sometimes very close to naturalism—without losing their unity. Christian art was less broadly based; the residues of a pagan art jostled it, so that it had to defend itself against their dissolving influence; but before that influence could prevail, the comprehension of traditional symbolism had first to become blurred. Nothing but an intellectual decadence, and more particularly a weakening of contemplative vision, can explain why medieval art later came to be regarded as "barbarous," clumsy, and poor.

Among the possibilities excluded by the spiritual economy of traditional Christian art is the representation of the nude. There are many representations of Christ crucified, as well as of Adam and Eve and of souls in hell or purgatory, but their nudity is, as it were, abstract and does not engage the attention of the artist. Be that as it may, the "rediscovery" of the naked body, considered as such and in its natural beauty, provided without doubt one of the most powerful springs of action of the Renaissance. So long as Christian art conserved its hieratic forms, surrounded by a folklore of decoration far removed from any concern with naturalism, the absence of the nude in art passed unnoticed, so to speak; icons were made, not to reveal this or that natural beauty, but to recall theological truths and to be the vehicles of a spiritual presence. As for the beauty of nature, of mountains, forests, or human bodies, it could be admired

Detail from Sandro Botticelli's
Birth of Venus, c. 1482

everywhere, outside the domain of art, all the more so because prudery, which grew up only with the urban culture of the fourteenth century, did not obsess the soul of the Middle Ages. Thus it was only when art began to try to imitate nature that the absence of "nudism" in medieval art came to be felt as a gap; but thereafter, the absence of any representation of the naked body could only be taken for prudery, and by the same stroke, the example of Greco-Roman statuary—not entirely unknown in the Middle Ages—became an irresistible temptation. In this connection the Renaissance appears as a cosmic retribution. It was perhaps dangerous to banish human beauty from the plastic arts—if indeed they already existed—human beauty being made in the image of God, but on the other hand one must not lose sight of the maleficent symbolism of "the flesh" in the Christian perspective and of the associations of ideas that might arise from this. Be that as it may, one can certainly not look to the Renaissance to confer afresh on physical beauty the sacred significance it held in certain ancient civilizations and still retains in India. The earliest and the most beautiful statues of the Renaissance, for example the *Fonte Gaia* of Jacopo della Quercia or the *David* of Donatello, have a tenderness that is still quite springlike, but they soon gave place to a Greco-Roman rhetoric devoid of content, and to a passionate expansivity which signifies "amplitude" only to a spirit bound to "this world." Nevertheless it sometimes happens that Renaissance sculpture is superior in qualities of nobility and intelligence to that of classical antiquity, and this can no doubt be explained by the influence of Christian experience, but it is by no means enough to confer on Renaissance art the slightest trace of traditional authenticity.

Similar considerations apply to the discovery of landscape in fourteenth century painting, and also, at a later period, of "open air," that is to say, the play of atmosphere and light. As subjects of artistic expression, each of these contains values precious in themselves and susceptible of becoming symbols—they function as symbols in other arts, particularly in the Far East—but Western art had discarded its sacred models, and lost its internal hierarchy, that formal principle that linked it to its traditional source. Indeed what makes the "desacralization" of art final and in a sense irreversible is not so much the choice of themes or subjects as the choice of formal language or "style."

There can be no better illustration of this law than the introduction into Renaissance painting of mathematical perspective, which is nothing but a logical expression of the individual point of view, that of the individual subject who takes himself as the center of the world. For if naturalism seems to capture the visible world as it is in its "objective" reality, it is because it has first projected the purely mental continuity of the individual subject onto the outer world. It makes that world poor and hard, and empty of all mystery, whereas traditional painting is limited to the transcription of symbols, while leaving to reality its own unfathomable depths. It is mathematical perspective, be it noted, centered on a single point that is here in question, and not a perspective of approximation, modified by occasional translocations of the optical center; such a per-

Jacopo della Quercia, *Fonte Gaia*,
Palazzo Publico, Siena

spective is not irreconcilable with an art having a spiritual foundation, for its purpose is not illusion but narrative coherence.

In the case of painters like Andrea Mantegna [*see* illustration page 104] and Paolo Uccello, the science of perspective became a real mental passion, a cold passion perhaps, and one not far removed from intellectual research, but destructive of pictorial symbolism: through perspective the picture becomes an imaginary work, and at the same time the world becomes a closed system, opaque to every gleam of the supernatural. In mural painting, a mathematical perspective is properly absurd, for it not only destroys the architectural unity of the wall, but also obliges the spectator to place himself on the imaginary visual axis, on pain of subjecting all the forms to a false foreshortening. In much the same way architecture is stripped of its most subtle qualities when the purely geometrical proportions of medieval art are replaced by arithmetical, and therefore relatively quantitative, proportions; in this respect the prescriptions of Vitruvius did much harm. It is here that one can see the pedantic character of the Renaissance: in losing its attachment to Heaven, it loses also its link with the earth, that is to say, with the people, and with true craft-tradition.

A rigorous perspective in painting inevitably involves a loss of color symbolism: by their dependence on an artificial illumination that goes hand-in-hand with spatial illusion, the colors lose their direct nature. A medieval painting is luminous, not because it suggests a source of light situated in the world depicted, but because its colors directly manifest the qualities inherent in light; they are glimpses of the primordial light that is present in the heart. The development of chiaroscuro, on the contrary, reduces color to nothing more than the play of an imaginary light; the magic of lighting carries painting into a sort of intermediate world analogous to a dream, a dream sometimes grandiose, but one that envelops the spirit instead of liberating it. Baroque art carried this development to an extreme, until finally spatial forms, suggested by chiaroscuro, lose the almost tangible corporeity conferred on them in Renaissance painting; at this point color seems to acquire an autonomous quality, but it is color lacking in sincerity, almost feverish, with a sort of phosphorescence that ends by devouring forms like a smouldering fire. Finally the normal relationship between

The Visitation, German manuscript, 12th century

form and color is reversed, so that it is no longer form, the graphic outline, that gives meaning to color, but it is color which, by its gradation, produces an illusion of volume.

II

So far as post-medieval sculpture is concerned, its illogicality—and its consequent incapacity to express transcendent essences—resides primarily in the fact that it tries to capture instantaneous movement, while its own material is static. Traditional sculpture accepts movement only in some of its more typical phases, themselves reduced to static formulations. A traditional statue, be it Romanesque, Hindu, Egyptian, or otherwise, always affirms the motionless axis; it dominates its environment by ideally relating it to the three-dimensional cross. With the coming of the Renaissance, and still more of the Baroque, the "sense of space" becomes centrifugal; in the works of Michelangelo for instance, it is like a spiral that "devours" space; his works dominate the surrounding void, not because they relate it back to its center, or to its omnipresent axis, but because they project into it their suggestive power, their magic spell [*see* illustration page 104].

At this point a possible misunderstanding must be forestalled. Autonomous statuary is a product of the Renaissance, or more exactly its rediscovery is; statuary detached from the body of a building is scarcely known in Christian medieval art. Sculpture which, in the guise of an independent column, dominates an architectural ambience or a landscape fashioned according to architectural principles, is fully in the spirit of Greco-Roman art; in Christian art, any such isolation of a sculptured figure would be close to idolatry. The fact is that sculpture expresses more

Saint Thomas Touching the Wounds of Christ, Monastery of Santo Domingo de Silos, Spain, early 12th century

Christ as Judge of the World,
Abbey Church of Sainte-Foy,
second half of the 12th century

completely than any other plastic art the principle of individuation, for it participates directly in the separative character of space; this quality is accentuated in a statue that is free on all sides. Christian art does not allow any such autonomy except to certain objects connected with worship, such as statues of the Virgin, crucifixes, or figured reliquaries. Statues which are not liturgical objects, such as those that adorn cathedrals, are almost always incorporated into the building; for the individual human form does not realize its full meaning save through its attachment to the form, both human and universal, of the Incarnate Word, and that form is represented by the sacred edifice, itself the "mystical body" of Christ.

There is however nothing absolute about this way of looking at things, nor is it common to all traditions. In Hindu art, for example, the independent statue is accepted; if one considers the principles of Yoga and the point of view it adopts towards the Divine Presence in man, it becomes clear that this must be so. Nevertheless, a close linkage between sacred sculpture and sacred architecture also exists in Hindu art, and it is in this aspect that it most closely approaches the art of the cathedrals.

The question of statuary brings us back to the subject that is fundamental to Christian art: the image of man. In the first place it is the image of God-made-man, and then that of man integrated in the Word, which is God. In the second case the individual form of man regains its original beauty by the very fact that it is reintegrated in the beauty of the Incarnate Word; this is expressed in the faces of the saints and prophets on the doors of cathedrals: the Face of the Christ contains them, they repose in Its "form."

In his masterly work *Verlust der Mitte* ("The Loss of the Center"), Hans Sedlmayr has shown how the decadence of Christian art, right up to its most recent phases, is above all a decadence of the image of man: the image of God-made-man, transmitted by medieval art, is succeeded by the image of autonomous man, of man glorifying himself, in the art of the Renaissance. This illusory autonomy implies from the first the "loss of the center," for man is no longer truly man when he no longer has his center in God; thereafter the image of man decomposes; first it is replaced, as regards dignity, by other aspects of nature, and then it is progressively destroyed; its systematic negation and disfigurement is the goal of modern art.

Here again we can discern a sort of "cosmic retribution." Just as the Incarnation of the Word has its corollary in the supreme sacrifice, and just as the "imitation of Christ" is not conceivable without asceticism, so the representation of the Man-God demands a "humility" in the means employed, that is to say, an emphasis on their remoteness from the Divine model. There is thus no true Christian art without a certain degree of "abstraction," if indeed it be permissible to use so equivocal a term to designate that which really constitutes the "concrete" character, the "spiritual realism," of sacred art. In short, if Christian art were entirely abstract, it could not bear witness to the Incarnation of the Word; if it were naturalistic, it would belie the Divine nature of that Incarnation.

III

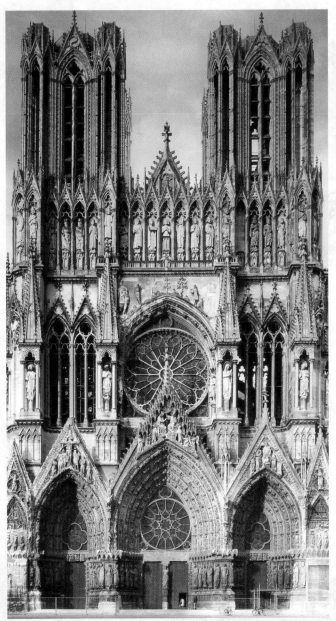

Like the bursting of a dam, the Renaissance produced a cascade of creative forces; the successive stages of this cascade are the psychic levels; towards its base it broadens out and at the same time loses unity and strength.

To a certain extent this fall can be detected even before the Renaissance properly so called, in Gothic art. The state of equilibrium is, in the West, Romanesque art and, in the Christian East, Byzantine art. Gothic art, more particularly in its later phases, represents a unilateral development, a predominance of the volitive element over the intellectual, an urge rather than a state of contemplation. The Renaissance can be looked on as a reaction, both rational and Latin, against this precarious development of the Gothic style. Nevertheless, the passage from Romanesque to Gothic art is continuous and without a break, and the methods of Gothic art remain traditional—they are founded on symbolism and on intuition—whereas in the case of the Renaissance the break is almost complete. It is true that not all branches of art run in parallel; thus, Gothic architecture remains traditional until its disappearance, whereas late Gothic sculpture and painting succumbed to naturalistic influence.

Thus the Renaissance rejects intuition, vehicled by symbolism, in favor of discursive reasoning, which obviously does not prevent it from being passional; on the contrary, because rationalism and passion go very well together. As soon as man's center, the contemplative

Cathedral of Reims, France, 13th century

intellect or the heart, is abandoned or obscured, his other faculties are divided among themselves, and psychological oppositions appear. Thus, Renaissance art is rationalistic—this is expressed in its use of perspective and in its architectural theory—and also passional, its passion having a global character: the affirmation of the ego in general, a thirst for what is big and without limit. Since the fundamental unity of vital forms still persists in one way or another, the opposition of the faculties continues to look like a free play; it does not yet seem to be irreducible, as it does in later times, when reason and feeling are separated by such a distance that art cannot contain them both at once. At the time of the Renaissance, the sciences were still called arts, and art still appears as a science.

Nevertheless, the cascade had been unleashed. The Baroque reacted against the rationalism of the Renaissance, the imprisonment of forms within Greco-Roman formulae, and their subsequent dissociation. But instead of overcoming these weaknesses by means of a return to the supra-rational sources of tradition, the Baroque sought to melt the congealed forms of Renaissance classicism into the dynamism of an uncontrolled imagination. It readily attaches itself to the later phases of Hellenistic art, the imagination of which is nevertheless much more controlled, more calm, and more concrete; Baroque art is animated by a psychic anxiety unknown to antiquity.

Baroque art is sometimes worldly and sometimes "mystical," but in neither case does it penetrate beyond the world of dreams; its sensual orgies and its gruesome *memento mori* are no more than phantasmagorias. Shakespeare, who lived on the threshold of that epoch, could say that the world was of "the stuff that dreams are made on"; Calderón de la Barca, in *La vida es sueño* ("Life is a Dream"), implicitly says the same thing; but both he and Shakespeare stood far above the level on which the plastic art of their time was developed.

The protean power of imagination plays a certain part in most traditional arts, especially in Hindu art; but here it corresponds symbolically to the productive power of *Maya*, the cosmic illusion. To a Hindu, the proteism of forms is not a proof of their reality, but on the contrary, of their unreality with respect to the Absolute. This is by no means true of Baroque art, which loves illusion; the interiors of Baroque churches, such as Il Gesù and St. Ignatius in Rome [*see* illustrations page 105], produce a hallucinatory effect; their cupolas, with their concealed bases and irrational curves, elude every intelligible standard of measurement. The eye seems to be absorbed by a false infinity, instead of reposing in a simple

Raphael, *The Betrothal of the Virgin*, 1504

and perfect form; the paintings on the ceiling appear to lie open towards a sky full of sensual and mawkish angels.… An imperfect form can be a symbol, but illusion and lies are not symbols of anything.

The best plastic creations of the Baroque style are found outside the domain of religion, in squares and fountains. Here Baroque art is both original and unsophisticated, for it has in itself something of the nature of water, like the imagination; it is fond of conches and marine fauna.

Parallels have been drawn between the mysticism of a St. Teresa of Ávila or a St. John of the Cross and a particular contemporary style of painting, that of El Greco for example; but at best such comparisons can be justified by the psychological conditions of the period, and more particularly by the religious ambience. It is true that this style of Baroque painting, with its magical effects of light, lends itself to the description of affective states that are extreme and exceptional; but this bears no relation to contemplative states [*see* illustrations page 104]. The very language of Baroque art, its identification with the psychic world, and with all that mirage of sentiment and imagination, prevents it from grasping the qualitative content of a spiritual state.

Nevertheless, while considering examples of the Baroque style, mention should be made of the strange reality of certain miraculous Madonnas. In their "modernized" forms they have generally been transformed by the hieratic costumes conferred on them by the people, enormous triangles of stiff silk and heavy crowns; only the face still exemplifies the Renaissance or Baroque style, but in the face, realism, carried to an extreme by the tinting of features and animated by the light of flickering candles, assumes the quality of a tragic mask. Here is something much more closely connected with sacred drama than with sculpture, reconstituted instinctively by the people, and appearing side by side with the art of the period, and in spite of it.

There are those for whom Baroque art represents the last great manifestation of the Christian vision of the world. This is no doubt because the Baroque still aspires towards a synthesis; it is even the last attempt at a synthesis of Western life on a foundation of any breadth. Nonetheless, the unity it achieves proceeds from an overweening will, which melts everything into its own subjective mold, rather than from an objective co-ordination of things in view of a transcendent principle, as was the case in medieval civilization.

In the art of the seventeenth century, the Baroque phantasmagoria congeals into rationally defined forms that are empty of substance; it is as if the

The Virgin of La Esperanza de Macarena, Seville, Spain

surface of the lava of passion were coagulated into a thousand hardened shapes. All later stylistic phases oscillate between the same two poles of passional imagination and rational determinism, but the greatest oscillation is that which took place between the Renaissance and the Baroque, all those that followed being lesser. But from another point of view, it is in the Renaissance and the Baroque taken together that the reaction against the traditional inheritance was manifested with the greatest violence; because, to the extent that art becomes historically more and more removed from this critical phase, it recovers a certain calm, a certain—though very relative—disposition towards "contemplation." It can nevertheless be observed that aesthetic experience is fresher, more immediate, and more authentic precisely where it is furthest from religious subjects: in a Renaissance "Crucifixion," for example, it may not be the sacred drama, but the landscape that manifests the higher artistic qualities; or in a Baroque "Entombment," it may be the play of light that is the real theme of the work—that is to say, the thing that reveals the soul of the artist—while the persons represented are secondary [*see* illustration page 104]. This is as much to say that the hierarchy of values has collapsed.

Throughout the whole course of this decadence, the individual quality of the artist is not necessarily the point at issue; art is above all a collective phenomenon, and men of genius who stand out from the crowd can never reverse the direction of an entire movement; at the most they can only accelerate or maybe slow down certain rhythms. The judgments made here on the art of the post-medieval centuries never take as a term of comparison the art of our times; that goes without saying. Renaissance and Baroque art had a scale of artistic and human values incomparably richer than anything that can be met with today. A proof of this, if proof be needed, is the progressive destruction of the beauty of our towns.

In every phase of the decadence inaugurated by the Renaissance, partial beauties are revealed, and virtues are manifested; but nothing of the sort can compensate for the loss of the essential. What does all that human greatness profit us, if the nostalgia for the Infinite that is innate in us is left without response?

IV

The succession of "styles" met with at the end of the Middle Ages can be compared to the succession of the castes that attained predominance in their respective periods. The word "caste" as used here means "human types," such as are in a sense analogous—though not parallel—to the different temperaments, and which may or may not coincide with the social rank normally occupied by each.

Romanesque art corresponds to a synthesis of the castes; it is essentially a sacerdotal art, but it comprises nonetheless a popular aspect; it satisfies the contemplative spirit, while responding to the needs of the simplest soul. Here is both serenity of intellect and the rough realism of the peasant.

Gothic art puts a growing emphasis on the spirit of chivalrous nobility, on a whole-hearted and vibrant aspiration towards an ideal. Though it has less "breadth" than Romanesque art, it still has a spiritual quality that is completely lacking in Renaissance art.

The relative equilibrium of Renaissance art is of an entirely rational and vital order; it is the congenital equilibrium of the third caste, that of merchants and craftsmen. The "temperament" of this caste is like water, which spreads horizontally, whereas nobility corresponds to fire, which surges upwards, consumes and transforms. The first caste, the sacerdotal, is like air, which is everywhere,

Clockwise: Miniature from the medieval Book of Hours, *Les Très Riches Heures du Duc De Berry*, 15th century; Ambrogio Lorenzetti, *Effects of Good Government in the City and the Country* (detail), 1338-1339; *Armed Knight*, 1335-1340; *Shops in a Covered Market*, miniature from the *Ethics* of Aristotle, 15th century

and invisibly gives life, while the fourth caste, that of the serfs, is like the heavy and motionless earth.

It is significant that the phenomenon of the Renaissance is essentially a "bourgeois" phenomenon, and that is why Renaissance art is as much opposed to popular art, as preserved in rural communities, as it is to sacerdotal art. Chivalrous art on the other hand, which is reflected in the Gothic style, never loses its direct connection with popular art, just as the feudal lord is normally the paternal head of the peasants in his fief.

It may be noted, however, that the equations: Gothic style = noble and warrior caste, Renaissance style = mercantile and bourgeois caste, are valid only in a broad sense, and are subject to all sorts of nuances. Thus, for example, the bourgeois and city-dwelling spirit, that of the third caste—whose natural preoccupation is the conservation and increase of wealth, both in the domain of science and that of practical utility—is already manifested in certain aspects of Gothic art; the Gothic was moreover the period of the development of urbanism. Likewise, although Gothic art is strongly impregnated with the chivalrous spirit, it is nonetheless determined

Abbey of Fontenay, France, 12th century

Cathedral of Reims, France, 13th century

as a whole by the sacerdotal spirit; and this is significant as regards the normal relationship between the first two castes. The break with tradition, and the loss of understanding of symbolism, came only with the supremacy of the bourgeois caste. But even here certain reservations must be made: the beginnings of Renaissance art are without doubt characterized by a certain sense of nobility; it could even be said that they show a partial reaction against the bourgeois tendencies manifested in late Gothic art. But this was only a brief interlude; in fact, the Renaissance was promoted by nobles who had become merchants and merchants who had become princes.

The Baroque style was an aristocratic reaction in bourgeois form, hence its pompous and sometimes suffocating aspect; true nobility loves forms that are clear-cut and light, virile and graceful, like those of a medieval coat of arms. Contrariwise, the classicism of the Napoleonic era was a bourgeois reaction in aristocratic form.

The fourth caste, that of the serfs, or more generally that of men tied to the earth, preoccupied with nothing but their physical well-being and devoid of social or intellectual genius, has no style of its own, nor even, strictly speaking, any art, if that word is used in its full sense. Under the rule of this caste, art is replaced by industry, which itself is the final creation of the mercantile and craftsman caste after it became detached from tradition.

V

Natura non facit saltus (nature does not make jumps), but all the same, the human spirit does "make jumps." Between medieval civilization, centered on the Divine Mysteries, and that of the Renaissance, centered on the ideal man, there is a deep cleavage, despite historical continuity. In the nineteenth century another cleavage appeared, perhaps even more radical. Up till then, man and the world around him still constituted an organic whole, at least in practice and in the domain of art which is here our concern; scientific discoveries, it is true, continually extended the horizon of this world, but the forms of everyday life remained within the "measure of man," that is to say, within the measure of his immediate psychic and physical needs. This is the fundamental condition under which art flourished, for art is the result of a spontaneous harmony between heart and hand. With the coming of industrial civilization, this organic unity was broken; man found himself confronted, not by maternal nature, but by lifeless matter, by a matter which, in the form of ever more autonomous machines, usurped the very laws of thought. Thus man, having turned his back on the

Baroque altar of St. Peter's, Rome, with the *Cathedra Petri* by Gianlorenzo Bernini, 1657-1666

Late Renaissance and Baroque: "The Tragedy of Christian Art"

From left to right: Michelangelo, *Victory*, 1532-1534; Gianlorenzo Bernini, *The Ecstasy of St. Teresa* (detail), Santa Maria della Vittoria, Rome, 1647-1652; El Greco, *St. Mary Magdalen in Penitence*, 1580-1586

"… In Rome, one clearly sees how Christianity was, as it were, bled of its spiritual aura by the Roman-pagan brutality, which it had never entirely overcome, and how after this sacrifice the ancient paganism rose up again, still more stupid and irrational than before, with a euphoria such as can only belong to a spiritual fall—not to mention the deviation of Christian influence in a suffocating and degraded 'mystique.'

"…Walking through the Vatican museums, I would have liked to outline a book then and there entitled: *The Tragedy of Christian Art*."

—from a letter by Titus Burckhardt to Frithjof Schuon, Oct. 24, 1950

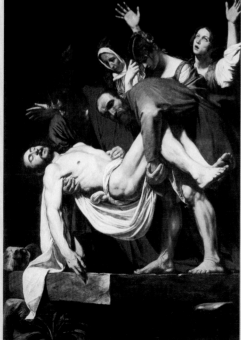

Caravaggio, *The Deposition*, 1604

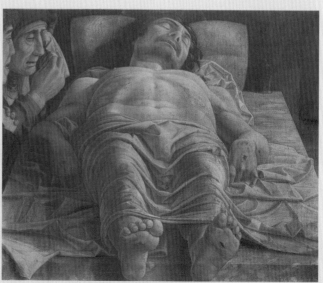

Andrea Mantegna, *Lamentation Over the Dead Christ*, c. 1490

Baroque vault of the Church of Il Gesù, Rome, 1676-1679

Baroque altar of St. Ignatius, Rome

immutable reality of the spirit—of "reason" in the ancient and medieval sense of the word—saw his own creation rising up against him like a "reason" external to himself, a "reason" hostile to everything which, in the soul and in nature, is generous, noble, and sacred. And man has submitted to this situation: with his new science of "economics," by means of which he hopes to maintain his mastery, he merely confirms and establishes his dependence on the machine. The machine caricatures the creative act, through which a supra-formal archetype is reflected into multiple forms, analogous one to another but never the same; the machine merely produces an indefinite number of strictly uniform copies.

The result of this is that art is uprooted from the soil that fed it; it is no longer the spontaneous complement of the craftsman's labor, nor the natural expression of a truly social life, but is thrust back into a purely subjective domain. As for the artist, he is no longer what he was at the time of the Renaissance, a kind of philosopher or demiurge; he is now a solitary seeker, without principle and without aim, unless indeed he is no more than the medium, or the clown, of his public.

This crisis broke out in the second half of the ninenteeth century; as at all historical turning-points, there was then a sudden and fleeting opening up of fundamental possibilities. With the rejection of naturalism, still connected as it was with the "homocentricity" of the Renaissance, the worth of "archaic" arts was recognized; it was understood that a picture is not an imaginary window looking out on nature, that the laws of painting are derived in the first place from geometry and chromatic harmony, and that a statue is not a figure frozen in full movement and by chance trans-

Paul Gauguin, *Orana, Maria*
("Salve, Maria"), 1891

formed into stone or bronze. The role of "stylization," the suggestive power of simple forms, and the intrinsic luminosity of colors were all discovered. At this moment a return to an art more honest, if not traditional art, seemed possible; in order to understand this, it is enough to recall some of Gauguin's pictures, or the reflections of Rodin on Gothic cathedrals and Hindu sculpture. But art no longer had either heaven or earth; it lacked not only a metaphysical foundation, but also an artisanal basis, with the result that artistic development rapidly bypassed certain half-open possibilities, and fell back into the domain of pure individual subjectivity—and did so all the more deeply because a universal and collective language was no longer imposed on it. Thrown back on himself, the artist sought new sources of inspiration. As Heaven was henceforth closed to him, and as the sensible world was no longer an object of adoration for him, he delved in certain cases into the chaotic region of the subconscious; in so doing, he released a new force, independent of the world of experience, uncontrollable by ordinary reason, and contagiously suggestive: *flectere si nequeo superos, acheronta movebo!* ("If I cannot move the celestial beings, I will stir up hell!"—Virgil, *Aeneid*, VII:312). Whatever it is that comes to the surface of the soul from out of this subconscious darkness, it has certainly nothing to do with the symbolism of the "archaic" or traditional arts; whatever may be reflected in these lucubrations are certainly not "archetypes," but psychic residues of the lowest kind; not symbols, but specters.

Sometimes this sub-human subjectivism assumes the "impersonal" demeanor of its congeneric antithesis, which could be called "machinism." Nothing could be more grotesque and more sinister than these machine-dreams, and nothing could more clearly reveal the satanic nature of certain features that underlie modern civilization!

VI

Let us now consider whether Christian art can be reborn, and under what conditions its renewal might be possible. First, let it be said that there is a certain chance, slight though it be, in the fact—negative in itself—that the Christian tradition and Western civilization are moving farther and farther apart. The Church, if it is not to be carried away in the chaos of the modern world, must retreat into itself. Some of its representatives are still trying to enlist the most modern and the most spurious artistic movements for the purposes of religious propaganda, but we shall soon see that anything of that kind can only accelerate the intellectual dissolution that threatens to engulf religion itself. The Church must have recourse to all those things that affirm its timeless nature; then only can Christian art return to its essential models and assume the role, not of a collective art permeating an entire civilization, but of a spiritual support; this will be all the more effective to the degree that it clearly opposes the formal chaos of the modern world. There are a few signs of a development in this direction; the interest in Byzantine and Romanesque art now appearing in religious circles may be mentioned as one of them. But a renewal of Christian art is not conceivable without an awakening of the contemplative spirit at the heart of Christianity; in the absence of this foundation, every attempt to restore Christian art will fail; it can never be anything but a barren reconstruction.

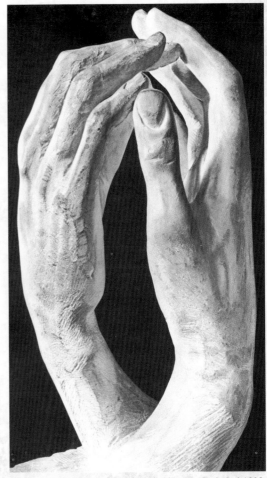

What has been said above about the principles of sacred painting lets us see the other conditions of its renewal. It is out of the question that Christian painting can ever be "abstract," that is to say, that it can legitimately be developed from the starting-point of purely geometrical symbols. Nonfigurative art has its place in the crafts, and especially in the art of building, where the symbolism is inseparable from the technical procedure itself. Contrarily to a theory that may be encountered in certain quarters, an image is not the outcome of a "gesture" made by the artist, but, on the contrary, his "gesture" proceeds from an inward image, from the mental prototype of the work. Whenever religious painting comprises a geometrical schematism, this has been superimposed on the image properly so called; the image remains the basis and substance of the art, and this is so for practical as well as for metaphysical reasons, since the image must not only be an anthropomorphic symbol, in conformity with "God become man," but also a teaching that is intelligible to the people. Painting, when considered in its technical aspects, no doubt partakes of the character of a craft, but this does not directly concern the spectator; in its

Auguste Rodin, *The Cathedral*, 1908

subject-matter and in its relation to the religious community, Christian painting must always be figurative. Abstract composition occurs only—and in its proper place—in ornament, thus constituting as it were a bridge between conscious and quasi-theological perception on the one hand, and unconscious and instinctive perception on the other.

Some maintain that the age during which a figurative religious art was necessary has come to an end, and that it is consequently impossible to "recapitulate" medieval Christian art; the Christianity of today, it is said, has come into contact with the non-figurative or archaic arts of so many different peoples that it could never recover an essential vision except in abstract forms, freed from all anthropomorphism. The answer to these people is that an "age" not determined by tradition has no voice in the matter, and above all that the anthropomorphism of Christian art is an integral part of Christian spiritual means, since it springs from traditional Christology; and besides, every Christian ought to know that a new "cycle" imposed from without can be nothing but that of the Antichrist.

The character of Christian painting is essentially, and not accidentally, figurative. This means that it can never dispense with the traditional prototypes that safeguard it from arbitrariness. These prototypes always leave a fairly wide margin for the exercise of creative genius, as well as for the special needs of times and places, in so far as these may be legitimate. This last reservation is of capital importance in a period when almost unlimited rights are attributed to "our times." The Middle Ages were not concerned with being "up to date," the very notion did not exist; time was still space, so to speak. The fear of being taken for a "copyist," as well as the search for originality, are very modern prejudices. In the Middle Ages, and to a certain extent even in the Renaissance and Baroque periods, ancient works, considered to be the most perfect in the period concerned, were copied; and in copying them, emphasis was quite naturally placed on those aspects that were seen as essential, and it is in this way that art is normally kept alive. In the Middle Ages especially, every painter or sculptor was in the first place a craftsman who copied consecrated models; it is precisely because he identified himself with those models, and to the extent that his identification was related to their essence, that his own art was "living." The copy was evidently not a mechanical one; it passed through the filter of memory, and was adapted to the material circumstances; likewise, if today one were to copy ancient Christian models, the very choice of those models, their transposition into a particular technique, and the stripping away from them of accessories, would in itself be an art. One would have to try to condense whatever might appear to be the essential elements in several analogous models, and to eliminate any features attributable to the incompetence of a craftsman, or to his adoption of a superficial and injurious routine. The authenticity of this new art, its intrinsic vitality, would not depend on the subjective "originality" of its formulation, but on the objectivity or intelligence with which the essence of the model had been grasped. The success of any such enterprise is dependent above all on intuitive wisdom; as for originality, charm, and freshness, these will come of their own accord.

ОА̇ БЛГВ КНЗЬ ДАНІ҇ИОСК:

Icon painting from the Danilov-Kloster, Moscow, 20th century

Christian art will not be reborn unless it completely frees itself from individualistic relativism, and returns to the sources of its inspiration, which by definition are situated in the "timeless."

Christ the Savior, Russia, 21st century

Illustrations

Frontispiece: *Carpet Page with Animal Interlace*, the Gospels of Saint Chad, early 8th century. Lichfield, Cathedral Treasury.

p. vi: *Carpet Page*, the Lindisfarne Gospels, late 7th century. Durham, Cathedral Library, A.II.17.

p. x: *The Beginning of the Gospel according to St. John*, Evangeliar from Trier, c. 1000. Manchester, John Rylands Library, Cod. 98.

INTRODUCTION TO THE SACRED ART OF CHRISTIANITY

p. xii: Altar fresco from the hermitage of Esquius, Vic, Spain, second half of the 12th century. Barcelona, Museo de Arte de Cataluña.

p. 3: The Christ-Logos as Creator, with Sophia, miniature from Flavius Josephus' *Antiquitates iudaici*, late 12th century. Paris, Bibliothèque Nationale, Cod. lat. 5047, folio 2r col. 1.

THE ROLE OF ILLUMINATED MANUSCRIPTS IN CHRISTIAN ART

p. 4: *The Evangelical Symbols*, the Book of Kells, folio 27v, early 9th century. Dublin, Trinity College Library, 58.

p. 7: *The Monogram Page*, the Book of Kells, folio 34r. Dublin, Trinity College Library, 58.

p. 8: The Book of Kells, detail from folio 250v. Dublin, Trinity College Library, 58.

p. 11: *Carpet Page*, the Book of Durrow, folio 85v, c. 680. Dublin, Trinity College Library, 57.

p. 12: *The Beginning of the Gospel according to St. John*, the Book of Durrow, folio 193r. Dublin, Trinity College Library, 57.

p. 13: *St. Mark the Evangelist*, Codex 51, detail from folio 78, Abbey Library of St. Gall.

p. 15: *Cross-Carpet Page Introducing the Gospel according to St. John*, the Lindisfarne Gospels, folio 210b. Durham, Cathedral Library, A.II.17.

p. 16: *Major Decorated Initial at the Beginning of the Gospel according to St. John*, the Lindisfarne Gospels, folio 211. Durham, Cathedral Library, A.II.17.

p. 19: Miniature XLVI, the Ambrosian Iliad, c. 5th century. Milan, Ambrosian Library.

p. 20: Detail of a miniature from the Codex Pupureus of Rossano depicting the parable of the wise and foolish virgins, 6th century. Reproduced in André Grabar, *Byzantinische Malerei*, Verlag Skira, 1953.

p. 21: *The Virgin and Child under a Canopy*, the Rabbula Gospels, folio Iv, 586. Florence, Biblioteca Medicea Laurenziana.

p. 22: *Canon Table*, Biblia Hispalense, folio 278r, 10th century. Madrid, Biblioteca Nacional.

p. 23: *Adoration of the Lamb*, Beatus Apocalypse, Santo Domingo de Silos, Spain, 1091-1109. London, British Library. Add. MS 11695, folio 86v.

p. 24: *Christ the Victor*, Beatus of Liébana, folio 151, 11th century. Soria, Biblioteca de la Catedral del Burgo de Osma.

p. 25: *Christ in Majesty*, Moralia In Iob of 945, folio 2. Madrid, Biblioteca Nacional.

p. 26: *The Heavenly Jerusalem*, the Apocalypse of Saint-Séver, 10th century. Paris, Bibliothèque Nationale, 8878.

p. 27: *The Heavenly Jerusalem*, the Morgan Beatus, 10th century. New York, Pierpont Morgan Library.

p. 28: *The Woman Clothed with the Sun, the Serpent, and the Child*, the Beatus of 975, folios 171 and 172. Gerona, Tesoro de la Catedral.

p. 29: *The Harvest of the Corn and the Grapes*, the Beatus of 975, folios 193v and 194r. Gerona, Tesoro de la Catedral.

p. 30: *Adoration of the Serpent and Beast*, the Beatus of 975, folio 215v. Gerona, Tesoro de la Catedral.

p. 31: *Letter Alpha*, the Beatus of 975, folio 216r. Gerona, Tesoro de la Catedral.

p. 32: *Angels Carrying the Gospel*, the Beatus of 975, folio 6. Gerona, Tesoro de la Catedral.

p. 33: *The Burning Babylon*, Beatus 975, folio 1215v. Gerona, Tesoro de la Catedral.

p. 34: *Jesus as the Lamb of God Standing on Mount Zion*, the Fanlo Beatus, c. 1000. New York, Pierpont Morgan Library.

p. 35: *The Triumphant Christian Warrior*, the Beatus of 975, folio 134v. Gerona, Tesoro de la Catedral.

THE FOUNDATIONS OF CHRISTIAN ART

p. 36: The Virgin of Vladimir, 12th century. Moscow, Tretyakov Gallery.

p. 38: *Masons and Sculptors*, French miniature, 15th century.

p. 39: The Christic monogram from the Catacombs, after Oskar Beyer.

p. 40: Christ as *Sol Invictus*, detail from the Mausoleum of the Julii, Rome, late 3rd century.

p. 41: Apse mosaic from St. Apollinare in Classe, Ravenna, c. 549.

p. 43: Crucifix from the Church of Santa Chiara, Assisi, 12th century.

p. 44: Cathedral of Monreale, 12th century.

p. 45: Church of Santa Constanza, Rome, 4th century.

p. 46: Central bay of the Royal Door, Chartres Cathedral, 12th century.

p. 47: The Royal Portal of Chartres Cathedral; The Door of the Virgin, right-hand tympanum of the Royal Door, 12th century.

p. 48: *Christ in Majesty*, fresco at the Abbey of Berzé-la Ville, early 12th century.

p. 50: Examples of the proportions of medieval churches, after Ernst Moessel.

p. 51: *Master Mason Supervising Stone Carving*; *The Scribe Eadwine*, from the Canterbury Psalter, c. 1150; *Sculptor*, bronze doors at the Church of San Zeno Maggiore, Verona; *Plowman at Work*, Flemish miniature, 14th century.

p. 52: *Goldsmiths*, Flemish miniature, 14th century; *A Painter*, English miniature, c. 1350; *Weavers*, Flemish miniature, 14th century.

p. 53: *Musician*, German miniature initial, 14th century; *Parchment maker*, German miniature initial, 13th century.

p. 54: *Dante and Beatrice Approaching the Sun*, Giovanni di Paolo, illumination for the *Divine Comedy*, folio 146r, Canto X, 15th century. London, British Library.

p. 55: *Demiurge* (God as Architect), miniature from the *Bible moralisée*, c. 1250. Vienna, Österreichische Nationalbibliothek, Codex Vindobonensis 2554.

p. 56: Wooden chest from Switzerland.

p. 57: Gargoyles in the Cathedral of St. Rumbald, Mechelen, Belgium; Gargoyle in Lichfield Cathedral, England.

p. 59: *The Medieval Universe*, after a French manuscript of the 14th century. Paris, Bibliothèque Nationale.

p. 60: *Boethius Discussing Music with Pythagoras, Plato, and Nichomachus*, 12th century. Cambridge University Library, MS I 1. 3, 12.

p. 61: *Personification of the Quadrivium* (four of the Seven Liberal Arts), from the *Arithmetic* of Boethius, c. 845. Staatliche Bibliothek, Bamberg, Class. 5.

p. 62: Ethiopian processional cross, 16th century. New York, the Metropolitan Museum of Art.

p. 63: First Lindau book cover, St. Gall, late 8th century. New York, Pierpont Morgan Library.

p. 64: Iconostasis, Cathedral of the Annunciation, Moscow, 1489; The original Byzantine plan of the Cathedral of St. Mark, Venice, after Ferdinand Forlati.

p. 65: Nave of the Cathedral of St. Mark, Venice, 1094.

p. 66: Nave of Sainte-Madeleine, Vézelay, France, 12th century.

p. 67: Crypt of Notre-Dame du Fort d'Étampes, Essonne, France, 12th century.

p. 68: Sainte-Chapelle, Paris, 1243-1248.

p. 69: Detail from the James the Greater stained-glass window, Chartres Cathedral, 13th century; Notre-Dame de la Belle Verrière, stained-glass window, Chartres Cathedral, 12th century.

p. 70: Different hieratic forms of the Cross.

p. 71: The "Cross of Victory," Oviedo Cathedral, Cámara Santa, Spain, 908.

p. 72: The Portal of St. Gall, Basle Cathedral.

p. 74: *The Mandilion*, Russian icon, Oslo, Collection Zeiner-Henriksen.

p. 75: *The Volto Santo*, Lucca.

p. 76: *Madonna and Child on a Curved Throne*, Greece, 13th century. Washington, D.C., National Gallery of Art.

p. 77: *The Great Panaghia*, Yaroslavl, 12th century. Moscow, Tretyakov Gallery.

p. 78: *The Holy Trinity*, St. Andrei Rublev, c. 1411. Moscow, Tretyakov Gallery.

p. 79: *The Ustyug Annunciation*, second half of the 12th century. Moscow, Tretyakov Gallery.

p. 80: *The Transfiguration*, School of Theophanes the Greek, Moscow, c. 1403. Moscow, Tretyakov Gallery.

p. 82: *The Virgin and the Child*, Basilica of St. Clare, Assisi, 12th century.

p. 83: Simone Martini, *Virgin and Child*, 1320. Town Hall, Siena; Simone Martini, *The Annunciation*, 1333. Florence, Uffizi Gallery.

p. 84: Icon of the Holy Face "Not Made by Hands" (*acheiropoietos*), School of Novgorod, Russia, 12th century. Moscow, Tretyakov Gallery.

p. 85: The Holy Virgin of the Sign, Greek icon. Pittsburgh, Pennsylvania, Collection George R. Hann.

p. 86: *The Nativity of Christ*, Novgorod, Russia, c. 1475; *St. Basil the Great*, Macedonia, 1699.

p. 87: *The Descent into Hell*. Workshop of Dionysius, Moscow, 1495-1504. St. Petersburg, Russian Museum.

p. 88: The Deesis, Pskov School, Russia, 13th century. St. Petersburg, Russian Museum.

p. 89: St. Tsarevitch Dimitri of Ouglitch, Russia, 17th century.

THE DECADENCE AND THE RENEWAL OF CHRISTIAN ART

p. 90: Cathedral of Strasbourg, West facade, 13th century.

p. 91: Three figures from the central portal of the West front, Chartres Cathedral, 13th century.

p. 92: Detail from Sandro Botticelli's *Birth of Venus*, c. 1482. Florence, Uffizi Gallery.

p. 93: Jacopo della Quercia, *Fonte Gaia*, Palazzo Publico, Siena.

p. 94: *The Visitation*, German manuscript, 12th century.

p. 95: *Saint Thomas Touching the Wounds of Christ*, Monastery of Santo Domingo de Silos, Spain, early 12th century.

p. 96: *Christ as Judge of the World*, Abbey Church of Sainte-Foy, second half of the 12th century.

p. 97: Cathedral of Reims, France, 13th century.

p. 98: Raphael, *The Betrothal of the Virgin*, 1504. Milan, Pinacoteca di Brera.

p. 99: The Virgin of La Esperanza de Macarena, Seville, Spain.

p. 101: Miniature from the medieval Book of Hours, *Les Très Riches Heures du Duc De Berry*, 15th century; Ambrogio Lorenzetti, *Effects of Good Government in the City and the Country* (detail), 1338-1339. Siena, Palazzo Publico, Sala dei Nove; *Armed Knight*, 1335-1340. London, British Museum; *Shops in a Covered Market*, miniature from the *Ethics* of Aristotle, 15th century. Bibliothèque de la Ville, Rouen.

p. 102: Abbey of Fontenay, France, 12th century; Interior of the Cathedral of Reims, France, 13th century.

p. 103: Baroque altar of St. Peter's, Rome, with the *Cathedra Petri* by Gianlorenzo Bernini, 1657-1666.

p. 104: Michelangelo, *Victory*, 1532-1534, Palazzo Vecchio, Florence; Gianlorenzo Bernini, *The Ecstasy of St. Teresa* (detail), 1647-1652, Santa Maria della Vittoria, Rome; El Greco, *St. Mary Magdalen in Penitence*, 1580-1586. Kansas City (Missouri), the Nelson-Atkins Museum of Art; Andrea Mantegna, *Lamentation Over the Dead Christ*, c. 1490. Milan, Pinacoteca di Brera; Caravaggio, *The Deposition*, 1604. Pinacoteca, the Vatican.

p. 105: Baroque vault of the Church of Il Gesù, Rome, 1676-1679; Baroque altar of St. Ignatius, Rome.

p. 106: Paul Gauguin, *Orana, Maria* ("Salve, Maria"), 1891. New York, the Metropolitan Museum.

p. 107: Auguste Rodin, *The Cathedral*, 1908. Paris, Musée Rodin.

p. 109: Icon painting from the Danilov-Kloster, Moscow, 20th century.

p. 110: *Christ the Savior*, Russia, 21st century.

Sources

"Introduction to the Sacred Art of Christianity": *Sacred Art in East and West*. World Wisdom, 2001, pp. 11-13, 15-16.

"The Role of Illuminated Manuscripts in Christian Art": *Famous Illuminated Manuscripts*. Urs Graf Verlag, 1964, pp. 3-30.

"The Heavenly Jerusalem": *Mirror of the Intellect*. State University of New York Press (SUNY), 1987, pp. 102-104.

"The Foundations of Christian Art": *Sacred Art in East and West*. World Wisdom, 2001, pp. 59-100.

"The Royal Portal": *Sacred Art in East and West*. World Wisdom, 2001, pp. 126, 129-130.

"Two Examples of Christian Symbolism": *Mirror of the Intellect*. SUNY, 1987, pp. 110-111.

"The Portal of St. Gall": *Sacred Art in East and West*. World Wisdom, 2001, pp. 105, 107, 119-120.

"Simone Martini": *Siena, The City of the Virgin*. Oxford University Press, 1960, p. 34.

"The Theological Message of Russian Icons": *Mirror of the Intellect*. SUNY, 1987, pp. 112-113.

"The Decadence and the Renewal of Christian Art": *Sacred Art in East and West*. World Wisdom, 2001, pp. 197-216.

"Late Renaissance and Baroque: 'The Tragedy of Christian Art'": Excerpt from a letter by Titus Burckhardt to Frithjof Schuon, 1950.

Index

Abgar, King, 74
Abraham, 75
Acheiropoietos, 74, 75, 84
Adam, 2, 42, 92
Aeneid, the, 20, 106
Alchemy, 69
Ambrosian Iliad, the, 19, 20, 111
Ammonius of Alexandria, 22
Andrei Rublev, St., 75
Anthropomorphic, Anthropomorphism, 39, 107, 108
Antichrist, the, 108
Apocalypse, the, 108
Apocalypse of Gerona, the, 28
Apocalypse of Saint-Séver, the, 26
Aristotle, Aristotelian, 54, 58, 59, 60
Asia, Asiatic, 23, 58
Augustine, St., 5, 42, 44

Baroque, 1, 68, 94, 95, 98, 99, 103, 108
Beatus, the, 23, 25, 26, 27, 32, 35
Beatus of Liébana, 26
Blacherniotissa, 75
Boethius, 60, 61
Book of Durrow, the, 10, 12
Book of Kells, the, 6, 10, 12, 14
Breviarium Mozarabicum, the, 5
Byzantine, Byzantium, 14, 18, 20, 21, 22, 47, 64,
    74, 78, 81, 89, 97, 107

Caesar, Julius, 40
Calderón de la Barca, 98
Carolingian, 9, 22
Catacombs, the, 39, 40
Celtic, 9, 10, 12, 20, 70
Charlemagne, 22, 25, 81
Charles V, 32
Chartres Cathedral, 46
Chiaroscuro, 94
China, 92
Chivalrous, 83, 100, 102
Christ, 2, 22, 23, 25, 31, 37, 40, 41, 42, 46, 47, 62,
    73, 74, 75, 77, 78, 79, 81, 82, 84, 86, 92, 96, 97
Christology, 49, 108
Classicism, 9, 98, 103
Codex Amiatinus, 18
Codex of Facundus, 28
Codex Rossanensis, 21
Constantine, Emperor, 40
Constantinople, 74, 75
Coomaraswamy, A.K, 1
Coptic Egypt, 23

Council of Seville, 23
Council of Trent, 62

Dante, 40, 47, 53, 54, 68
Donatello, 93
Didascalia Apostolorum, 5
Dionysius the Areopagite, 79, 82
Durant de Mende, 44
Durham Gospels, the, 17
Durrow Gospels, the, 12

Eadfrith, 17, 18
Eastern Church, the, 67
Echternach Gospels, the, 13, 17
Egypt, 2, 22, 23, 39, 40, 69, 91, 95
Eidos, 1, 58
El Greco, 99
Elipandus, 23, 25
Emeterius, 32
Eucharistic, 62, 64
Euclid, 5
Eusebian Canon, the, 22
Eve, 92

Florence, 18, 22, 83
Fonte Gaia, 93
Forma, 50, 54, 58, 59, 81

Gall, St., 13, 14, 73
Gargoyles, 57
Gauguin, Paul, 106
Genesis, 2
Gnosis, 39
Gospels of St. Chad, the, 13
Gothic, 67, 73, 97, 100, 102, 103, 106
Goya, Francisco de, 35
Graeco-Roman, 37, 39
Greek, 1, 18, 20, 39, 58, 62, 64, 77, 82
Guénon, René, 51, 54

Hellenism, 82
Henry VIII of England, 6
Hermes Trismegistus, 2
Hesychast, 82
Hierotheos, St., 81
Hindu, 44, 46, 49, 50, 58, 95, 96, 98, 106
Homer, 20
Honorius d'Autun, 44
Hyle, 50, 58, 59, 60
Hylemorphic, Hylemorphism, 59, 60

Iconoclasm, 21, 22
Iconoclast, 78, 81

Ignatius St., 98
Il Gesù, 98
Iliad, the, 20
Incarnation, 81, 97
Insular, 12, 18
Intellect, 50, 51, 60, 64, 98, 100
Ireland, 6, 9, 10, 21
Irish Script, 9
Isidore of Seville, 60
Islam, 22, 78
Itala Fragments of Quedlinburg, 20

Jerome, 9
Jerusalem, 26, 27, 70
Jews, Jewish, Judaic, 38, 52
John Damascene, St., 81

King Ferdinand I of Catalonia, 28
Koran, 25

Lesser Mysteries, the, 54
Libri Carolini, 81
Lindisfarne Gospels, the, 13, 14, 17, 18
Logos, the, 25, 50, 60

Mandilion, 74
Mantegna, Andrea, 94
Martini, Simone, 83
Materia, 47, 50, 54, 58, 59, 60, 61
Materia prima, 51, 47, 50, 58, 59, 60
Maya, 98
Mesopotamia, 21
Michelangelo, 95
Moors, 23, 32
Moses, 42
Mozarabic, 22, 23, 25, 28

Napoleon, 35, 103
Nicea, VII Council of, 79, 81
Nicodemus, 74
Northumbria, 13

Origen, 44
Orthodox, 40, 64, 75, 82

Palaeo-Christian, 75
Palladium, the, 29
Pantheon, the, 39
Pantocrator, 31
Paradiso, 47
Pater Emeterius, 32
Patriarchs, the, 19, 42, 86
Patrick, St., 19
Persia, 22, 26

Plato, Platonic, 59, 60
Priscian, 13
Prophets, 19, 42, 86, 96
Proportion, 61
Protean, Proteism, 1, 98
Purgatorio, 54
Purusha, 44, 46, 49
Pythagorean, 37, 49, 60

Quadrivium, the, 60

Rabbula Gospels, the, 21, 22
Rodin, Auguste, 106
Roman Empire, 22, 40
Romanesque, 5, 57, 67, 70, 73, 95, 97, 100, 107

Sacramentarium Leonianum, 5
Santiago de Compostela, 32
Santo Domingo de Silos, 27
School of Cluny, 32
Schuon, Frithjof, 52, 104
Sedlmayr, Hans, 96
Shakespeare, 98
Shekhina, 42
Solomon, 42
Sutton-Hoo, 14
Symbolism, 1, 38, 42, 44, 46, 49, 50, 51, 54, 56, 58, 61, 64, 73, 75, 79, 81, 84, 86, 92, 93, 94, 97, 103, 106, 107
Syria, 6, 21, 22, 23, 74

Tabor, 82
Teresa of Ávila, St., 99
Theodore of Studion, 81
Theotokos, 22
Tibet, Tibetan, 10, 58
Toledo, 23, 25, 27

Uccello, Paolo, 94

Vajra, 50
Vatican, the, 104
Vatican Virgil, the, 20
Venice, 64
Vergilius Romanus, the, 20
Vienna Genesis, the, 21
Virgil, 5, 20, 53, 106
Virgin Mary, the, 22, 83
Visigothic, 23, 25, 32
Volto Santo, 74
Vulgate, the, 17

Yoga, 96

Zorobabel, 42

Biographical Notes

TITUS BURCKHARDT, a German Swiss, was born in Florence in 1908 and died in Lausanne in 1984. Burckhardt was an eminent member of the "traditionalist" or "perennialist" school of twentieth century thought, devoting his life to the study and exposition of the different manifestations of the timeless wisdom—the *philosophia perennis* or *sophia perennis*—underlying the world's great religions.

Although Burckhardt was born in Florence, he was the scion of a patrician family of Basle, Switzerland. He was the great-nephew of the famous art historian Jacob Burckhardt and the son of the sculptor Carl Burckhardt.

Burckhardt was fluent in German, French, Arabic, and English and wrote 17 books in German, eight books in French, translated three books from Arabic into French, and wrote numerous articles in various languages. Twelve of these books have been translated into English. A more extensive biography and a complete bibliography are available on www.worldwisdom.com.

The Best Summary of Titus Burckhardt's Life and Writings:

The Essential Titus Burckhardt: Reflections on Sacred Art, Faiths, and Civilizations,
edited by William Stoddart, World Wisdom, 2003

Other Books by Titus Burckhardt on Christianity and Sacred Art:

Siena, City of the Virgin, Oxford University Press, 1960
Mirror of the Intellect, State University of New York Press, 1987
Chartres and the Birth of the Cathedral, World Wisdom, 1996
(Revised edition forthcoming in 2007)
Sacred Art in East and West, World Wisdom, 2001

KEITH CRITCHLOW is Professor Emeritus at the Prince of Wales Foundation in London and co-founder of the Temenos Academy. He was a former professor of Islamic Art at the Royal College of Art and Founder Member of the Research into Lost Knowledge Organization. He is the author of books on geometry, anthropology, the principles of Islamic design, and the Neolithic origins of architecture. His works include *Islamic Patterns: An Analytical and Cosmological Approach*, *Order in Space*, and *Time Stands Still*.

MICHAEL OREN FITZGERALD has written and edited numerous publications on world religions. His book *Christian Spirit* was named "Best Book on Religion & Philosophy for 2004" by the Midwest Independent Publisher's Association. Four of his books on American Indian spirituality are used in university classes. Fitzgerald has taught Religious Traditions of the North American Indians in the Indiana University Continuing Studies Department at Bloomington, Indiana. He holds a Doctor of Jurisprudence, cum laude, from Indiana University. Michael and his wife, Judith, have spent extended periods of time visiting traditional cultures and attending sacred ceremonies throughout the world.

Other Titles on Christianity by World Wisdom

Christian Spirit,
edited by Judith Fitzgerald and Michael Oren Fitzgerald, 2004

The Destruction of the Christian Tradition: Updated and Revised,
by Rama P. Coomaraswamy, 2006

For God's Greater Glory: Gems of Jesuit Spirituality,
edited by Jean-Pierre Lafouge, 2006

The Fullness of God: Frithjof Schuon on Christianity,
selected and edited by James S. Cutsinger, 2004

In the Heart of the Desert: The Spirituality of the Desert Fathers and Mothers,
by John Chryssavgis, 2003

Not of This World: A Treasury of Christian Mysticism,
compiled and edited by James S. Cutsinger, 2003

Paths to the Heart: Sufism and the Christian East,
edited by James S. Cutsinger, 2002

Paths to Transcendence: According to Shankara, Ibn Arabi & Meister Eckhart,
by Reza Shah-Kazemi, 2006

The Sermon of All Creation: Christians on Nature,
edited by Judith Fitzgerald and Michael Oren Fitzgerald, 2005

Ye Shall Know the Truth: Christianity and the Perennial Philosophy,
edited by Mateus Soares de Azevedo, 2005

Other Titles in the Sacred Art in Tradition Series by World Wisdom

The Feathered Sun: Plains Indians in Art and Philosophy,
by Frithjof Schuon, 1990

Frithjof Schuon on Universal Art: Sacred and Profane,
edited by Catherine Schuon, 2007

Images of Primordial and Mystic Beauty,
by Frithjof Schuon, 1992

Sacred Art in East and West,
by Titus Burckhardt, 2001